Catholic Bushido

Catholic Bushido™

Transformational Virtue — The Way of the Catholic Warrior

By Joseph A. Daczko

Follow on Twitter @CatholicBushido

www.facebook.com/Catholic-Bushido-1098964200276813/

This book is dedicated to my wife Angela - without you in my life virtue would have been just another word - and to my sons Nathaniel David and Joseph Vandell - I love you and pray that you will always fight for goodness and holiness, especially in your own lives, but also in the world around you. Be strong always.

Acknowledgements

I would like to thank all of my family and friends who have supported me in the writing of this book. Special thanks go first to my wife Angela who is my inspiration and always my first proofreader. I would also like to thank my brothers in Christ, Don and Doug Engelhart for reading the early versions and giving me great feedback. Thanks also goes to Fr. John Denberger O.C.S.O. from the Abbey of the Genesee in Piffard, New York and to Fr. Ed Stafford, pastor of St Joseph's parish in Mantua, Ohio. Thanks also to Paul Wonders for all of his editing help. You all gave me great feedback and are clearly a part of this work. Thank you.

Table of Contents

1

Introduction

The smoke is black, thick, and hot; it billows out in greasy undulating clouds while flames pour from the doors and windows. The stud frames that were once pale, grained, and sound now glow an angry red. It won't be long now before the house falls. But a little girl remains inside. "She's only six!" her mother screams. While the girl's father is restrained by two paramedics, a volunteer fireman runs into the house. He's running into a death trap. Why? Because a person is in there, another life. He prays that he can get her out.

Less than twenty-four hours later, the same fireman is called to a convenience store parking lot. It's another overdose, and he's seen so many. As he walks up to the car, he hears the cries of a child, and his eyes take in the whole scene. A grown man and woman, both with seatbelts attached, are slumped over, eyes closed. A little girl still strapped in her car seat cries as she looks from one to the next. His heart breaks as he wonders what will happen to this young child, one that he cannot save.

We read these two stories and without personally knowing any of those involved our hearts are moved; we feel admiration and disgust, taking joy in the great potential for humanity, then grieving as we consider how far humanity can fall. We look at one scene, admiring someone who would risk his life for another, and then look at the other with a mixture of disgust and pity for two individuals who lost their way and left a vulnerable child behind.

Why do these stories provoke such strong reactions in us? Because deep inside the human spirit there is something that recognizes and discerns good from evil. There is an unquenchable and indestructible ember of God's truth that attracts all of us to goodness and beauty. It doesn't manifest itself in the same way for each individual, but it's there. When we hear stories of courageous virtue, personal sacrifice, or unselfish love, we don't even need to know the people involved to feel a burst of admiration. Our response demonstrates that this ember of truth and goodness runs deeper than any human relationship.

The Truth that Unites Us

The existence of objective goodness is recognized even outside the confines of churches and religious institutions. In her TED Talk "Why Some People are More Altruistic than Others," Abigail Marsh explains that the drive to be altruistic (defined as showing a selfless concern for the well-being of others) is different for each individual.[1] Humanity exists along a "continuum of altruism" from not very altruistic to highly altruistic. Specific parts of our brains are tied to our individual levels of altruistic potential. This means that altruism is not just some abstract choice we make, but rather it is a part of our physical and created bodies. In a study conducted by psychologists Katherine Dahlsgaard and Christopher Peterson, the authors found that "there is convergence *across time, place, and intellectual tradition* about certain core virtues."[2] They state that this convergence suggests a nonarbitrary foundation for the classification of human strengths and virtues. They identified six core virtues in all: courage, justice, humanity, temperance, wisdom, and transcendence.

We can reasonably argue, then, that there seems to be a generally shared sense of goodness and right character among all people. And I think that most of us would likely agree just based on our own personal lives and relationships. The foundation of this goodness appears to be, to use Dahlsgaard and Peterson's word, "nonarbitrary," meaning not subject to individual determination. It gives us the idea of something fundamental, something that is there whether or not we choose it to be.

I would give a name to this nonarbitrary foundation of goodness: Jesus Christ. All of Scripture proclaims this message that all goodness in us and in the world comes from God. In the first chapter of the book of Genesis, we read that when God created the world, "it was good." That same book tells us that He created us in His image and likeness. So, from the moment of our conception, each one of us has been created good. And similar to how an artist marks his work, this generally shared sense of right character is God's "signature of goodness" written on every heart and mind across the globe throughout the ages.

Knowing that there is a shared goodness among all people brings me great joy and great hope. **Goodness exists and is a part of our very being!** We have been made for it, and it can **never** be wiped away. As faith-filled people, we believe this. We believe that goodness wins in the end—not because Hollywood movies have conditioned us to expect this, but because we've already experienced the endurance of goodness. It is a goodness with depth and strength, not just a good feeling that rapidly leaves us like the blowing wind. We can sense this goodness acting like the bedrock or cornerstone of our being. It is something that fits into us like a puzzle piece. Unlike in the movies, this goodness—this hopefulness—is not an emotion or event. It is not a "happily ever-after" end to a story that can potentially be changed, destroyed, or ruined by tragedy. No, this goodness is the kind that weathers the storms of tragedy and difficulty, is not tied to emotions, and will always be there. Because it is God's creation, it can never be destroyed.

This affirmation of our innate goodness is a joyful and hopeful message we all need. But as this message comes to us, we look out into society and see that we don't always act from this goodness. Why not? Because there is also sin in the world. Our sin. Sin that works to keep us from opening this gift of goodness and achieving the end for which we were created.

Our Goal

Men, we have each been created good by God. We have been made for a reason and with purpose. Each one of us, as Catholics, has been given a great responsibility to consciously acknowledge this gift of ours. One which has been given to us by a father who loves us without limit. By acknowledging that our goodness is a gift, we simultaneously admit that it must be used—or else some piece of us will go unfulfilled. In other words, we have to not only appreciate goodness but do good ourselves. Sometimes when we recognize the need to act, we search about for special opportunities, perhaps serving for a day at a soup kitchen or clothing center. I applaud this impulse and would like to encourage it—but I believe our real challenge is much more basic and hits us closer to home. Our goal isn't to make goodness an occasional or even frequent interruption of our regular life—but to let it permeate everything we do. We must strive, while fully relying on God's help and grace, to live out of the goodness we have been given. To work to encourage a greater development and unfolding of God's goodness inside of us so that it can displace sinful behavior, continuously making us into new people according to God's intended design. When this becomes our goal, the entire journey of our lives will contain more goodness, especially those normal times that exist between planned moments of charitable action.

As we purposefully strive to live a life based on God's goodness, our will seeks Him out and moves into closer alignment with His will. In this position of closer alignment with God, it is much more likely that His ultimate plan for us will be accomplished. And ultimately, this should be the goal of all baptized Christians.

The *Catechism of the Catholic Church* says that "only in God will man find the truth and happiness he is searching for" and that "God never ceases to draw man to himself."[3] So as we are striving to allow more of His goodness to develop and unfold in our lives, we recognize that we are relying fully on God's grace to pull us forward. Any change that we experience is of His design; it is a spiritual development and movement as God draws us from our current individual state of being and directs us toward Himself, who is our ultimate end. We are engaged in a continuous process of transformation from our personal human weakness to spiritual strength, from being a slave to becoming an heir. Galatians 4:7 says, "So you are no longer a slave but a child, and if a child then also an heir, through God."

It Is a Battle

Day by day, as we go about living our lives, we sometimes (or often) struggle to do the right things because of sin. Within each of us there is a war raging—a war between virtue and vice. Virtue is defined as a quality considered morally good or desirable in a person; vice is moral depravity or corruption.[4] In the year AD 405, Aurelius Prudentius Clemens wrote "The Battle for the Soul of Man (Psychomachia)."[5] This epic poem describes the battle that rages within us daily by bringing to life both the virtues and the vices in the form of warriors on a battlefield. In it, for example, Chastity battles and defeats Lust, and Patience defeats Wrath. This poem helps us to see that not everything in life is gray; some things are black and white. There is evil in the world, and we must recognize it. But there is also an overwhelming amount of good, which counteracts evil. Across time and across the world, this battle between good and evil has been fought. But as we join the fight, we do not compete against an outside opponent; the conflict is happening inside each one of us. The battle is against the evil of our own fallen nature.

When engaged in any war, victory depends on strong warriors who are well trained and willing to act. But these warriors cannot win by performing any action they choose; they must perform specific actions determined by an established code shared among all their fellow warriors.

The samurai warriors of feudal Japan followed a standard code of conduct known as Bushido. This code was based on seven virtues that each warrior was expected to exemplify: honesty, courage, respect, benevolence, rectitude, honor, and loyalty. The Bushido code provided context and focus to the application of the samurai's martial strength. The samurai was expected to use his skill and power to promote the development and protection of social order. A samurai who failed to live by a code of virtue and gave in to vice was disgraced and cast out of his community, unfit to hold his former station. As

Christian people fighting battles of our own, we too have been given a code of virtue to help direct us.

The Code of the Catholic Warrior

Years ago, I attended Mass at the Cathedral of the Madeleine in Salt Lake City, Utah. After the priest's homily, a thought struck me: In addition to the saving and redeeming nature of His death and resurrection, Jesus made "being human" worth something more than it was before His birth. He redeemed the experience of human life and elevated its value by living human life Himself. Our humanity and the life that we live here on earth has greater meaning simply because Jesus Christ chose to be one of us.

I believe this "elevation" also occurs with respect to the created goodness that God has put into all people. In society today, people like to say, "What's really important is that you're a good person." I think they are unconsciously appealing to the universal foundation of virtue and goodness that God gave to us all. It's true, we all recognize and appreciate acts of goodness. However, we have to think deeper. What does it mean to "be" a good person? "To be" is much different than "to act like" or to do good things. As a human being who was created in the image and likeness of God, but one who also has a sinful nature, for me to "be" good is to be deeply changed and transformed. The aforementioned seeds of goodness and virtue that were planted in humanity require redemption through the saving action of Christ. **Goodness and virtue must become more than just ways of acting; they must become ways of being so that they draw us along the path toward our Creator.**

We are fully in need of God's grace to accomplish any of this. As Christ has said, "Apart from me you can do nothing" (John 15:5). And so our church, not government or society, helps us and presents to us seven foundational virtues. We can learn to understand and practice some of these virtues on our own, while others (faith, hope, and love) are infused into us by God's grace alone. In this light, the virtues are not just a code of behavior for personal good—and not merely the way in which we order a good and just society—but by God's grace they spiritually transform us. By faith in God, while trusting in His grace, and through practice of these virtues, we take daily steps on our path towards sanctity. It is by walking and staying on this path that we are most disposed to hearing God's call, which will guide us to become who we are truly and most deeply meant to be.

Our walk with God is not just about what we do. It is about who we are and who we are becoming in Christ. We must align our human will and our freedom to choose with the path of right acting that God and His church have outlined for us; then we must let God lead us where He will.

The Virtues

The *Catechism of the Catholic Church* outlines seven fundamental virtues from which all other virtues flow. The seven are separated into two groups: the cardinal virtues and the theological virtues. The cardinal virtues are prudence, justice, fortitude, and temperance.[6] These virtues can be acquired on our own by education and practice. By deliberately choosing to be just, we further develop the virtue of justice in ourselves, and so on. The theological virtues, sometimes referred to as the infused virtues, are faith, hope, and love. These virtues cannot be acquired by our own individual efforts. They are gifts of God and infused into us solely as a gift of His grace. However, once the seeds of these virtues have been planted in us, it is our responsibility to foster their growth.

The practical value of the virtues is that they provide to us a set of godly behaviors that we can consciously strive to emulate. As men, we typically want to take action, and the virtues give us something toward which we can apply our energy. They can serve as a focal point of daily prayer and action. The beautiful mystery of this is that while we are willfully striving to actively practice the virtues, God will be with us, coaching us along the way as a true Father would. In this activity, we move ourselves into a place of surrender to God, and it is in these moments of willful surrender to God's direction that we are best disposed to hearing His special call that is for each one of us alone. As a result, not only does our behavior become more "virtuous," but we are transformed; God's creative design for each of us, which is found only in our surrender to Him, is allowed to operate. Over time, with patience and diligence, this practice can transform our way of being, and it may very well influence other people in our lives. As Catholic men who are battling daily and need clear direction, the cardinal and theological virtues become our code— the code of the catholic warrior. Our code calls us to surrender our own will and submit to the practice of transformational virtue: this is Catholic Bushido.

Catholic Bushido

God has granted you the gift and the responsibility of free will. You have the power of choice. If you choose to live according to God's will, He gives you the grace, courage, and strength you need to accomplish the tasks He has in mind for you alone. It is your responsibility to acknowledge your own sinfulness while also acknowledging the gift of reconciliation. You are called to willfully choose to do good daily—to fill yourself with goodness and leave no room for sin. How you are to do it depends on God's specific design for your life.

Your responsibility is also to go into this task of right acting with the appropriate spirit—one of surrender to God's will and design for you. The practice of the virtues is simply meant to help you maintain the attitude of surrender to Him, thereby increasing the probability of hearing or sensing the nudging of the Holy Spirit as He moves in the quiet depths of your heart.

Prayer

Be lifted up, O child of God. Rejoice in your Father's love for you. Know that you are valued and needed; you were created for a reason, for a purpose that only you can accomplish. Be filled with courage and sing your song aloud, **a song of war and a song of joy**—joyful that the battle has been won, and thankful that you can be called a son. Amen.

Scripture for Reflection

"God created mankind in his image; in the image of God he created them; male and female he created them."

—Genesis 1:27

"God looked at everything he had made and found it very good. Evening came, and morning followed—the sixth day."

—Genesis 1:31

"I urge you therefore, brothers, by the mercies of God, to offer your bodies as a living sacrifice, holy and pleasing to God, your spiritual worship. Do not conform yourselves to this age but be transformed by the renewal of your mind, that you may discern what is the will of God, what is good and pleasing and perfect."

—Romans 12:1–2

"So then, my beloved, obedient as you have always been, not only when I am present but all the more now when I am absent, work out your salvation with fear and trembling. For God is the one who, for his good purpose, works in you both to desire and to work."

—Philippians 2:12–13

"Put on the armor of God so that you may be able to stand firm against the tactics of the devil. For our struggle is not with flesh and blood but with the principalities, with the powers, with the world rulers of this present darkness, with the evil spirits in the heavens. Therefore, put on the armor of God, that you may be able to resist on the evil day and, having done everything, to hold your ground. So, stand fast with your loins girded in truth, clothed with righteousness as a breastplate, and your feet shod in readiness for the gospel of peace. In all circumstances, hold faith as a shield, to quench all [the] flaming arrows of the evil one. And take the helmet of salvation and the sword of the Spirit, which is the word of God."

—Ephesians 6:11–17

"We know that all things work for good for those who love God, who are called according to his purpose. For those he foreknew he also predestined to be conformed to the image of his Son, so that he might be the firstborn among many brothers."

—Romans 8:28–29

"What then shall we say to this? If God is for us, who can be against us?"

—Romans 8:31

"No, in all these things we conquer overwhelmingly through him who loved us. For I am convinced that neither death, nor life, nor angels, nor principalities, nor present things, nor future things, nor powers, nor height, nor depth, nor any other creature will be able to separate us from the love of God in Christ Jesus our Lord."

—Romans 8:37–39

Wisdom of the Saints

"Since it is likely that, being men, they would sin every day, St. Paul consoles his hearers by saying 'renew yourselves' from day to day. This is what we do with houses: we keep constantly repairing them as they wear old. You should do the same thing to yourself. Have you sinned today? Have you made your soul old? Do not despair, do not despond, but renew your soul by repentance, and tears, and Confession, and by doing good things. And never cease doing this."

—St. John Chrysostom[7]

"He who goes about to reform the world must begin with himself, or he loses his labor."

—St. Ignatius of Loyola[8]

"The life of a Christian is nothing but a perpetual struggle against self; there is no flowering of the soul to the beauty of its perfection except at the price of pain"

—St. Padre Pio[9]

Questions for Reflection

1. What are all of the ways in which God has made His creation good?

2. What is the goal of the Christian life? Is this your goal?

3. Can you think of any other virtues besides the four cardinal virtues and the three theological virtues? Name them and see how they relate to any of the primary seven.

4. What does the *Catechism of the Catholic Church* say about virtue?

5. Does practicing the virtues guarantee our holiness and salvation? Why or why not?

6. In what ways would a more diligent practice of the virtues change your life?

2

The Seven Deadly Sins

The Ailments That Trap Us

Put yourself in the position of a person who struggles with an unidentified ailment. Day after day, he feels terrible, not knowing what comes next or if his pain will ever end. It weighs him down physically, of course, but also mentally, emotionally, and spiritually. Why? Because humans are created as integrated beings with body, mind, and spirit.

The different facets of our being are interconnected, with each separate part affecting the other: the physical affects the spiritual, the emotional impacts the mental, and so on. In the case of a person with an undiagnosed illness, part of his struggle is that he feels trapped in a dark box with no visible exit. How can there be hope or confidence in a return to health if the "thing" remains a mystery? This is why we have doctors. We go to them in search of a name for our ailments. We ask them to identify our sickness and to prescribe a path to healing. This process removes the box's top and shows us a way out. Now we can see a path in front of us and feel that we can finally take action and move forward. At this point hope is enkindled, providing our weak humanity with a boost of strength to fight for our health—and in some cases to fight for our lives.

In her historical and collective wisdom, and through the grace of Jesus Christ, Holy Mother Church functions as a physician for our souls here on earth. Through the writings of John Cassian, Pope Gregory the Great, and others, she has identified for us a list known as the seven capital vices (or the seven deadly sins).[1] The Catechism says that these sins are capital because they serve as the foundation for other sins. The difference between the church and a doctor, however, is that the church works with us throughout our lifetimes to form our consciences so that *we* learn to know the illnesses' identities. The church helps us to recognize and name the ailments that may be affecting our own soul. Once we can name the illness of our soul, we can receive guidance and take action in fighting it. The action prescribed generally starts with humble confession; then, through the grace we receive, we daily choose the way of sanctity rather than of sinfulness. Healing and renewal, after all, are the point of the Sacrament of Reconciliation. Unlike the way the Catholic Church is sometimes portrayed, she does not name the seven capital vices in order to look around society and point out our offenses with a long, bony, accusing finger. **She knows that each of us, on our individual paths to sanctity, needs healing and must be able to humbly acknowledge our own sins**. The *Catechism of the Catholic Church* quotes St. Augustine in saying that "God created us without us: but He did not will to save us without us."[2]

The Seven Capital Vices (Deadly Sins)

The part we play in our healing is to place our hope in God's grace as we learn to recognize vice and how it seeks to ensnare us. Sin and vice act as a clamp on our souls. As we fight against these oppressors, we open our hearts to the true love that God has for us. When we can release and let go of our selfish drives, our souls unclench. Then, like a hose with the clamp removed, God's love and grace flow freely through us and out to others. This is when we are most satisfied with our lives and most filled with joy.

The seven deadly sins are lust, gluttony, greed, sloth, wrath, envy, and pride. Notice that they encompass the physical as well as the emotional, mental, and spiritual aspects of human behavior. Although all of these are capital sins, they are not equal in their destructive potential. They are listed above in order of increasing severity, starting with lust and culminating with pride. Let's look at them now in greater detail.

Lust (unfettered sexual desire)

Okay, so let's get this out of the way in very clear and straight-forward language. The Catholic Church is **not** against sex or the enjoyment of it. The church is opposed to the **disordered** desire for sex. That is what lust is. "Lust is *disordered* desire for or *inordinate* enjoyment of sexual pleasure. Sexual pleasure is morally disordered when sought for itself, isolated from its procreative and unitive purposes."[3]

Disorder is defined as disturbing the normal or regular functioning of something. In the case of lust, this means disturbing the normal, regular functioning of our sexual behavior. But what do these disruptions look like? Examples include a man (or woman) sitting at a computer at 3 AM watching pornography while everyone else is asleep; a computer seized by police with explicit images of child pornography; a serial rapist being convicted of violating over a dozen women; a mother of three divorcing her husband over an extramarital affair; a single man with eight children, all with different mothers; a work colleague who cannot stop talking about sex; or a man who, despite being a father to a young daughter, visits a strip club. Lust can be at work behind the scenes driving any number of behaviors. There is one key element of lust we must recognize: it always harms other people beyond the one engaging in the vice. In each of the examples above, notice the other parties affected. There are wives, co-workers, vulnerable children, and victimized women. As much as we might want to think otherwise, sinful actions rarely, if ever, have no effect on others.

As men, we know that lust likes to attack us through who and what we see. In the Gospel of Mathew, Jesus says, "You have heard that it was said, 'You shall not commit adultery.' But I say to you, everyone who looks at a woman with lust has already committed adultery with her in his heart" (5:27–28). Jesus points it out to us right there: "if we look at a woman with lust…" The sin of lust is not in seeing something, but in looking. Sight happens, but looking is intentional.

In our world today, images that can provoke men into lustful thoughts are everywhere. The newsstand, the checkout line at the grocery store, movies, television, smartphones, social media feeds, or the ads on a webpage. But take heart! The sin is not about the first glimpse; it is about what we do immediately upon seeing the provocative image. Do we avert our eyes? Do we stop thinking about what it was we saw? (Yes, this is difficult, but we can push it out with a different thought.) Years ago, a parish priest described to me the practice of "taking custody of the eyes." This is willful action to control what we look at. When an image appears, willfully choose to take control or "custody" of your eyes—and look away. Practice this technique the next time you are out in public or at the store. You can stay out of the traps lust sets for you, but you have to be vigilant. Once you name this sickness of lust and recognize it for what it is, you can marvel at the absurdity of the tradeoff being offered to you. Is a single sexual experience worth more than decades of happiness with your wife and family? Let me answer that for you: No!

Questions to Ask Yourself:

- Can I abstain from sex for a period of time without issues in my marriage?
- Do I get mad at my spouse when she does not want to have sex with me? If so, why?
- What is the first thing I think when I see someone of the opposite sex? What is the second thing I think?
- Do I hide any sexual behaviors?
- Would I want my daughter to be involved in the pornography industry? How about my wife or mother? Why or why not?
- How much responsibility does the viewer or consumer of pornography have in the exploitation of the men, women, girls, and boys who are featured in this material?

Scripture for Reflection

"Avoid immorality. Every other sin a person commits is outside the body, but the immoral person sins against his own body. Do you not know that your body is a temple of the holy Spirit within you, whom you have from God, and that you are not your own? For you have been purchased at a price. Therefore, glorify God in your body."

—1 Corinthians 6:18–20

Gluttony (over-indulgence)

Gluttony is overindulgence in food or drink. Eating and drinking are good and necessary activities; their purpose is to keep us alive and to keep our bodies and minds strong and functioning properly. It is also appropriate to celebrate and have parties and feasts that feature different types and quantities of food and drink. A glutton, however, is one who eats and drinks for pleasure alone. Perhaps he consumes an excessive quantity of food; or maybe he indulges on the costliest entrees and vintages. At the end of the day, a glutton's mind becomes fixated on food or drink as an end or goal unto itself. Like lust warps sexuality, gluttony creates a disordered view of food and drink.

In the United States, gluttony manifests itself culturally through the epidemic of obesity. In the year 2000, the National Institute of Health stated that the epidemic of obesity was reaching critical proportions, classifying an estimated 250 million people worldwide as obese.[4] More recently, the *Cleveland Plain Dealer* published an article stating that 39.8 %—basically four out of every ten Americans—are obese.[5] Now, widespread obesity may be a modern phenomenon, but gluttony is not new. Our Holy Mother Church has many things to share with us about this vice if we would quietly listen for a moment. For instance, John Cassian wrote about gluttony during his lifetime more than 1,500 years ago (AD 360–435).

What does gluttony look like? Not in terms of people's body shape or figure—I mean, how are gluttonous thoughts and disorders manifested in the lives of people? Habitual overeating is one obvious example. And gluttony shows itself in those that will only eat or drink the most expensive brands—

"only the best." Working in corporate America, I often encounter people who search after and talk about the best wines and spirits, buy them for several hundred dollars a bottle or order expensive after-dinner whiskeys, and then brag to colleagues about it. This is not to say that having a wine or whiskey collection is sinful, but one should certainly consider how much mental and emotional energy is sunk into this hobby and make sure things are in balance. When out for a business dinner, how does a healthy person deal with these situations? What is the right course of action? Is it possible not to be pulled along in this thought process?

We have to look for the right balance. With a mind "disordered" by gluttony, we may consider it unremarkable for business dinners to be comprised of $70 prime steaks and $300 bottles of wine. If at a business dinner in an expensive restaurant, then order as modestly as you can and then move on. We can't change our environment, but we can control our behavior within it. I know that on many occasions where I have traveled for work, especially when I am alone, I will simply choose to eat simply, going to a place like Chipotle, rather than having a longer sit-down meal. I personally do this even though company policy allows us to spend a much greater amount.

We have also strayed from the maxim of cleaning our plates that many of our parents and grandparents grew up with and tried to teach us. The amount of food we put on our plates, don't eat, and throw away is another subtle action involving gluttony. We see a significant amount of appealing food and put more on our plates than we could ever finish. Next time you are at the Chinese buffet, only put on your plate what you know with certainty you will finish. If you have room for a little more once this is consumed, then go up a second time. Just do this in moderation.

Eating and drinking is, for most people, a pleasurable experience, and I believe that God designed it to be this way. But just like lust disorders how we function sexually, we can develop a disordered appetite. There may be psychological reasons for our gluttonous behavior, but it is still disordered and we need healing. Many times, in addition to physical, mental, or emotional healing, we also need spiritual healing. And that's okay; if we need it, we should look for it. Galatians 5:1 says, "It is for freedom that Christ has set us free." I know that this verse is chiefly concerned with freedom from the dictates of the laws governing Jewish faith, but when I read it I cannot help but believe that this also relates to so many of our human compulsions—Christ wants us to be free of those as well.

Questions to Ask Yourself:

- Do I care if people know what brand of food or drink I consume?
- Am I always thinking about food or drink?
- Can I refuse or stop myself from taking a second or a third helping?
- Do I brag about the places I eat or how expensive they were?
- Must I always have certain kinds of drinks, snacks, or treats in my house?

Scripture for Reflection

"Now look at the guilt of your sister Sodom: she and her daughters were proud, sated with food, complacent in prosperity. They did not give any help to the poor and needy."

—*Ezekiel 16:49*

"Do not join with wine bibbers, nor with those who glut themselves on meat. For drunkards and gluttons come to poverty and lazing about clothes one in rags."

—*Proverbs 23:20–21*

Greed (avarice)

In this life, where does your consolation come from? In what do you find security for today and for your future? In my case, I work a day-to-day job in the corporate world. In this world I meet and know a lot of very compassionate and helpful people—people that have hearts for helping others. And in many ways, my hope is strengthened through these encounters. In my experience, there are many more good people in this world than bad.

On the flip side, I have also known some people who behave quite differently. Almost every act seems to be calculated to help themselves advance in position, power, income, or all of the above. It is one thing to seek out a promotion for the betterment of a growing family, but some people refuse to be satisfied no matter how lofty their title or salary.

I have been in discussions with colleagues where the conversation turns to future opportunities, and some of these folks list positions they would like to have. In today's corporate environment, this is not abnormal. Many young people today look to change jobs regularly (as frequently as 18–24 month intervals) in order to move up in position as quickly as possible. Little attention is paid to how well they performed the previous job or what measurable contributions they made to the organization. It is all about moving up. It seems to me that this is a subtle form of greed: to seek out something that we don't have for its own sake. We look to this thing or position as the item that brings consolation, security, and joy to our life, when that should be God's role. As in all things, a modest desire for career growth and success is not bad. It becomes vice when the desire corrupts and disorders our character.

Can people with comparatively little money or material things be greedy? This vice manifests itself differently in people of contrasting social status, but everyone is at risk. For those in an impoverished situation, a fixation on obtaining and hoarding resources may feel like a matter of survival. But this mindset can lead into sin. I believe the thing to consider here is that our current state of life does not make us immune to certain vices. Wealthy people can be greedy, but people with little or no money can be greedy too. Greed is a matter of who we are, not what we have.

Questions to Ask Yourself:

- Do I want more of something I already have in abundance?
- Do I feel unsatisfied with my home? My job? My title?

- Will I hoard certain items? If I have many, will I make sure that I get more, even at the expense of someone who has none?
- Can I or do I try to distinguish between my needs and my wants?
- Do I ever think of other's needs? What do I do about the needs of others?

Scripture for Reflection

"Let your life be free from love of money but be content with what you have, for he has said, 'I will never forsake you or abandon you.'"
—*Hebrews 13:5*

"Then he said to the crowd, 'Take care to guard against all greed, for though one may be rich, one's life does not consist of possessions.'"
—*Luke 12:15*

Sloth (laziness/idleness)

Does this word conjure up images of a two or three-toed furry mammal moving slowly up a tree branch? Because of how slowly they move, sloths are named after one of the seven capital vices, the one associated with laziness. I wonder how they feel about that?

To get at the heart of what sloth is, let's look at Leon J. Suprenant's paraphrase of Fr. John Hardon's definition. Sloth is "sluggishness of soul or boredom because of the exertion necessary for the performance of a good work. The good work may be a corporal task, such as walking; or a mental exercise, such as writing; or a spiritual duty such as prayer."[6] Sloth is not simply failing to complete tasks on time, but it encompasses the mental, emotional, and spiritual attitude that precedes the thing not being done. It is the attitude behind the lack of action.

Over my lifetime, especially as a younger man, I have struggled with this vice. I remember having chores to do and doing the least amount possible to be able to say I did it—always looking for the simplest and fastest way out. This inner attitude even followed me into my first couple of jobs as a teenager. The thing is, I don't think the tendency for laziness ever leaves us fully, and it can flow into our spiritual lives. For example, I usually read Scripture every morning before going to work, but there are times that I just read the chapter or the verses in order to check the box that I did it, rather than to read Scripture in order to know God better and more intimately. I have also fought the vice in the writing of this book. The thought and idea for this work first hit me several years before I actually started writing it. Some of that delay stemmed from not being sure if it was really something God wanted (I have to admit I still wonder on this point), but on another level I wasn't ready to commit myself to the work and study required to make it happen.

We should also be aware that sloth is not always presented as a decision to do or not to do; sometimes it works by presenting an "alternative." In our culture today, we are over-entertained. Maybe we should call it "uber-tained" because everything seems to push us toward entertainment. We are constantly presented with things that keep us from being bored. Many of these distractions come at us through screens—big screens, small screens, medium screens, personal screens, family screens, and theater screens—from cinemas to TVs to phones to tablets. Certainly you know all too well the danger to productivity due to these omnipresent screens. It is so easy to fall into social media, video games, or any number of other distractions. How often do you sit down on your couch and pull up Facebook rather than a real book? I am not suggesting these things in themselves are bad or evil; however, when they promote an attitude of procrastination, when you keep telling yourself, "I'll get to it later," then your technology is supporting the vice of sloth. Just ask the college freshman who is on Twitter rather than studying biology.

Does this attitude of "just not feeling like" praying ever impact you? Does it stop you from going to church or the men's group meeting? This is the vice of sloth impacting your spiritual life. I personally have experienced feeling this disinclination prior to church meetings. At times like these, our enemy, the devil, is trying to corrupt our desire for rest to keep us from an experience of spiritual enrichment. When I overcome the vice and force myself to attend these gatherings of my Christian community, I find that in the majority of these instances the specific meeting or event notably blesses my soul.

Questions to Ask Yourself:
- Do I feel an internal resistance to doing spiritual things?

- When the thought of reading Scripture or other spiritual books or articles comes, does it feel like a heavy weight has been placed on my shoulders?
- Do I make excuses when someone invites me to a men's meeting, to Mass, or to a prayer group?
- Do I justify myself with those excuses? Is it someone else's fault that I am not going to the meeting or reading the book?

Scripture for Reflection

"The appetite of the sluggard craves but has nothing, but the appetite of the diligent is amply satisfied."

—*Proverbs 13:4*

"Do not grow slack in zeal, be fervent in spirit, serve the Lord."

—*Romans 12:11*

Wrath (anger)

So, who has never been angry? No one. Everyone gets angry. The sin of wrath and anger is not about the emotion itself. It's about what we do with our anger and how we do it. The biblical example of holy anger we all like to point to is Mark 11:15–19 where Jesus overturns the money changers' tables in the temple. This passage justifies all of our angry actions, right? In this passage, however, Jesus was in full control of Himself; He knew exactly what

He was doing and why. On the flip side, the vice of wrath is not defined by a feeling of anger or a justifiable response to an unjust situation. Like other vices, this one too is disordered and leads to uncontrolled behavior. Does your anger go from zero to 100 miles per hour in 0.4 seconds? Do you "lose" your mind and not think rationally when angry? This loss of control is the vice. When we lose control, we tend to say or do things that are likely not in proportion to whatever made us angry in the first place. In Exodus 21:23–25, the command is given regarding recompense for a personal injury: "But if injury ensues, you shall give life for life, eye for eye, tooth for tooth, hand for hand, foot for foot, burn for burn, wound for wound, stripe for stripe." I wonder if the people in Jesus' time considered this passage as license to act vengefully. But it seems likelier that the concept of "an eye for an eye" was intended to limit wrath rather than permit a certain level of vengeful action. Either way, to make sure we really got it, Jesus goes even further in the Gospel of Mathew and says to turn the other cheek rather than retaliate (Mathew 5:38–40).

I personally have struggled with the vice of wrath. I have found that wrath tends to explode when I have too many things going on at once, and then one of those things does not go as planned, or something unexpected gets added on top. So most of the time I become irrationally angry because my expectations are not met—in short, I have lost control of the situation.

You may have heard the expression of going home and kicking your dog; well, I can tell you there have been times where I have been irrationally mad at my own dog (especially when she was a puppy). Her name is Pepper and she is a Great Dane. When she was a puppy, she was 125 pounds of energy and rambunctiousness, so much so that one of our living room windows took the brunt of her interaction with a chair. I am a dog person, and I love this dog, but there are times when I really want to wring her neck. The irony is that she tends to be especially irritating to me when I am trying to be peaceful. For example, in my prayer life I like to have times of silence and solitude. But just when I start to feel the calm coming on—that's her cue to start doing all manner of dog things such as growling at the car driving down the road or barking at the plastic bag blowing through the back yard. This pulls me back out of prayer, interrupting my desire for quiet prayer time, and I get irritated. This is a holy anger, right? Perhaps not. As I reflect on these events, I notice that the true source of my irritation and anger is the fact that I am "not getting what I want," which was the peaceful time in prayer. So instead of that peace, I get filled with an irrational anger.

In St. Alphonsus Liguori's work entitled "On the Sin of Anger," he quotes St. Bonaventure in saying that an angry man is unable to distinguish what is just and unjust.[7] During my prayer time, can I really fault my dog for acting like...a dog? No, I can't. Apply this same thought to a husband and wife having an argument where both of them are yelling and speaking out of anger. What is the likelihood that the object of this argument will be resolved without hurt feelings? Or how about an uncontrolled, angry outburst when you are the only one angry? How does this affect others around you? In their eyes, are you still a just man, one to be trusted? All vices, including anger, will swiftly take control of our mental, emotional, and physical faculties when we passively allow this to happen.

Questions to Ask Yourself:

- Do you go from 0 to 100 mph on the anger scale immediately?
- Have you ever been ashamed of an angry outburst after the fact?
- Have others been ashamed of you after an angry outburst?
- Have others, especially those close to you, told you that you need to get a handle on your anger?
- Have you ever struck anyone from anger?
- Can you recognize when an angry outburst is imminent and move away from it?
- Do you always need to be in control?

Scripture for Reflection

"Be angry but do not sin; do not let the sun set on your anger, and do not leave room for the devil."

—Ephesians 4:26–27

"Know this, my dear brothers: everyone should be quick to hear, slow to speak, slow to wrath, for the wrath of a man does not accomplish the righteousness of God."

—James 1:19–20

Envy

"The Lord looked with favor upon Abel and his offering, but on Cain and his offering He did not look with favor. So, Cain was very angry and dejected" (Genesis 4:4–5). What happens next? Cain kills his brother Abel because Abel received favor from God. Favor that was not given to Cain. Cain was envious, and it drove him to murder.

Envy and jealousy are two distinct vices. Envy is spiritual and emotional sadness on account of something that another possesses that we want for ourselves. Jealousy, on the other hand, is discontent provoked by someone else's success; we worry that what we have will be taken from us because of that person's success. In either case, our total focus is on ourselves. We feel that the success of another somehow makes us "less" in some way. Envy may even tempt us to take action in order to "lessen" the other person by taking away what they have. For example, envy could arise when a co-worker receives an award that they deserve based on performance. Desiring to have that award or promotion is not bad if it causes you to improve your performance and try to fairly earn it on your own. The vice enters in when you downplay the other's success, perhaps saying, "John really only won that award because he let all his other responsibilities slide."

The tenth commandment says that you must not covet anything that belongs to your neighbor. Exodus offers a list of examples of what not to covet, which includes your neighbor's house, wife, servants, and livestock. In today's world, we might substitute car, house, position, office, telephone, and even recognition. The vice of envy is a direct attack on charity and love of neighbor. Envy divides people. Rather than rejoicing in our neighbor's success, envy causes us to plot against our neighbor's efforts, thinking that by tearing him down we lift ourselves up and become better in the process. This is obviously an unbalanced way of thinking. However, it can also subtly worm its way in without us knowing. We can even be envious of another person's friendships or position in social circles—even in the church.

Questions to Ask Yourself:
- How do I feel when a co-worker, friend, or relative is promoted or honestly earns accolades for themselves?
- Can I willfully and publicly congratulate and praise another person?
- Do I pray for others and for their greater success?
- Do I talk in terms of *we did* or *I did*? Do I acknowledge and elevate the role others play? Or do I downplay them as I describe my own efforts?
- If there is a person that on the surface I feel I do not like, why is that? Is envy at the root of my dislike?

Scripture for Reflection

"A tranquil heart gives life to the flesh, but envy makes the bones rot."

—*Proverbs 14:30 (ESV)*

"For where jealousy and selfish ambition exist, there is disorder and every foul practice."

—*James 3:16*

Pride (vanity)

The *Catechism of the Catholic Church* defines pride as "an inordinate self-esteem or self-love, which seeks attention and honor and sets oneself in competition with God."[8] Does this mean it is bad to love yourself? No, but here again we see the word "inordinate." Vices are always inordinate and go to the extreme. An inordinate self-love becomes sinful when it does not acknowledge the gifts of other people in our lives and keeps us from loving them.

Because we are regularly inundated with outside stimuli, watching others' lives through television, print media, social media, and so on, it has become easy for us to point out pride and arrogance in others when we see and hear it. We see it in the worlds of sports, politics, and entertainment. We see it everywhere. We categorize pride as being this rude "I am better and I know better" attitude that is openly flaunted before us. Although these are examples of pride at work, I sense in myself sometimes that because I have so many opportunities to point it out in others, it leaves me with less time to point out pride in myself. I am not talking about the over-the-top self-promotion prevalent in the worlds of celebrities and professional sports, but rather the subtle forms that pride takes in my daily life.

As with most vices, pride tends to isolate and divide. I can become so convinced of my superiority in worldly or spiritual things that I don't listen to others, and so unconsciously I fail to interact with others in human, loving, and meaningful ways. The truth of this struck me when I took part in a men's renewal program at our local parish. As part of the renewal process, men get up in front of the attendees and tell their faith story. During this particular renewal, I was sitting in the back listening to a man give his witness, but I was really not paying attention. The man talking at this time had a learning disability, and you could tell by the way he talked. Initially, as he spoke, my own pride and arrogance had closed my ears. But as I listened, an insight (or the Holy Spirit's 2x4) struck me: there was something that I could learn from this man. I had to admit that my own ears were closed to what he had to say because my pride said, subconsciously, that I was smarter than him. Pride was keeping me from truly listening to and knowing this man. This is a lesson I have to take to every corner of my life: be vigilant not to tune people out because of my subconscious feelings of superiority.

I have also seen this vice at work in groups of people. In the corporate world where organizations are divided up between research, marketing, and sales functions, I have seen firsthand how each group thinks they know best how to set strategy and move forward as an organization. When individual pride and then even functional "group" pride sets in, no one wants to listen to the other; we are only silent in order to wait for our opportunity to speak. We see this in our current social and political climate as well. Pride is running rampant throughout our various political spheres no matter our party affiliation or demographic group. Whenever I as an individual believe I know all about a topic, and no one can tell me anything to help me rethink or even adjust my opinion, then pride has come home to roost.

Questions to Ask Yourself:

- When someone's talking to me, am I thinking about my response, or am I listening and trying to understand what they mean?
- Are there any areas in my life in which I consider myself to be an expert? Do I believe it? Do I want everyone to believe it?
- Am I worried about receiving credit for all of my actions?
- Can I be taught? Can I listen to criticism? Do I immediately defend myself when someone shares criticism?
- Do I *desire* God's will to be done in my life, without my control?

Scripture for Reflection

"Pride goes before disaster, and a haughty spirit before a fall."

—*Proverbs 16:18*

"But he bestows a greater grace; therefore, it says: 'God resists the proud, but gives grace to the humble.'"

—*James 4:6*

"For by the grace given to me I tell everyone among you not to think of himself more highly than one ought to think, but to think soberly, each according to the measure of faith that God has apportioned."

—*Romans 12:3*

Naming our ailments (or vices) is the first step we can take toward healing and living a life of grace with our Lord. But the healing does not come simply through naming the ailment—we must then choose and follow the correct treatment plan. In other words, our healing requires action. Using our modern view of medicine as an analogy probably falls a little short here because our typical view is to expect the doctor to give us a pill that will cure our ailment. We prefer to take a pill to lower our cholesterol rather than change our diet and commit to regular exercise. This removes from us any specific responsibility for our own healing. At this point, returning to the analogy of a battle may be more appropriate for continuing our discussion of virtue and vice.

The Psychomachia

Around AD 405, an epic poem entitled "The Psychomachia (the Battle for Man's Soul)" was written by Prudentius Aurelius Clemens.[9] This work is not overly long, but it gives us some insight into the real battle between virtue and vice. I recommend reading it. The entire poem is written as a battle scene, and so expect some violent imagery, such as when Faith cuts off the head of the "worship of the old gods."

As the poem unfolds, Faith is the first virtue to step onto the battlefield. This makes sense; in order for us to want to be in this battle, we must believe in God. The next virtue is Chastity, and the vice Lust comes to fight her armed with torches. The vice tries to thrust these torches into the eyes of Chastity. We see again here how Lust attacks, targeting our eyes as our weak point.

The virtue of Patience then takes the field in her quiet manner, never even changing expression. Wrath sees her from a distance and, according to the poem, is enraged. Weapons are thrown at Patience, but she stands unharmed as they fall at her feet. "Patience waits because Wrath will perish by her own violence"—and indeed wrath commits suicide. Patience helps all of the other virtues in their battles. In this, we see that in reality our battle is not just one vice versus one virtue, but it is good versus evil. The virtues all work in complementary ways and are bound together. In the same way, the vices build one upon another and complicate the battle.

Pride now comes to the field of battle riding around on a prancing horse. She and her horse are all puffed up with their own greatness. She expects her enemies to bow down before her, but Lowliness and Hope stand firm. Through this section of the poem, Pride scorns a number of other virtues and talks down to them, including Sobriety, Purity, Fasting, and others. In the end Pride rides, without thinking and at full gallop, across the battlefield toward her enemies. But the vice Deceit has dug a pit and into this pit Pride's horse stumbles; the vice is thrown from her horse. Lowliness and Hope approach her and cut off her head.

The next vice to come forward for battle is Indulgence, who throws baskets of flowers over her enemies, and her sweet breath sucks the courage out of the virtues. Sobriety comes to their aid and delivers a long passionate plea to the virtues. Her plea references many of the biblical stories of old, of those who struggled and won holiness. Last but *not* least, she reminds them all of the cross of Christ and His sacrifice as she raises it high into the air. Vice will attack us by promising pleasure and comfort.

Many other vices come onto the battlefield, such as Greed and her friends Anxiety, Perjury, Fraud, Sordidness, and others. Some of the vices can change and take on seemingly good forms and bring death through treachery. So the battle continues and the virtues continue to fight. Towards the end of the poem, the author directs a prayer to Christ: "It was your wish that we find the dangers in us and recognize the struggle which our hearts endure. We know, now, that in our murky hearts conflicting loves battle." This prayer coincides with James 1:14–15: "Rather each person is tempted when he is lured and enticed by his own desire. Then desire conceives and brings forth sin, and when sin reaches maturity it gives birth to death."

This is our battle, the battle that has been fought for eternity, raging in each one of us. We may not be warriors in the physical sense, but we must fight in the spiritual sense. Our way to engage in battle is not just to try to "stop" doing wrong, but to **do right**. The way that we drive darkness from an unlit room is by filling it with light. In the same way, let us fill our hearts, our minds and souls, and our world with virtue.

Consider Matthew 12:43–45 with vices and virtues in mind:

> "When an unclean spirit goes out of a person it roams through arid
> regions searching for rest but finds none. Then it says, 'I will return to
> my home from which I came.' But upon returning it finds it empty,
> swept clean and put in order. Then it goes and brings back with itself
> seven other spirits more evil than itself, and they move in and dwell
> there; and the last condition of that person is worse than the first."

I cannot help but think what would have happened if that person, once he was
rid of the first evil spirit, had filled himself with virtue, rather than staying
empty.

The samurai warriors of feudal Japan were fiercely dedicated to their lord
and their responsibility. As Catholic men, we must be just as fiercely dedicated
to our place in time and to our responsibilities. We must enter into the battle
knowing our code and our way of fighting. Men of God, let us stand together
and fight for our God, for truth, for goodness, for our friends, our wives, our
sons and daughters, for all of the people we come into contact with each day,
and for the generations in our families that will come years and decades from
now.

Practice the virtues that we will study in the following chapters. Hold onto
them; willfully remember them. Go back frequently and read about them
here, in the Catechism, and in other works. Let us start the work of building
virtue piece by piece into our lives. When our lives are filled with the light of

virtue, it will shine through our actions and in our words. It may only shine through in simple and small ways. But we will shed light into people's hearts without them even knowing it. In doing this, it will be as if we are fanning the embers of goodness in their hearts. And who knows? In some, those embers may burst into flame. They will then take up the fight and spread it to others. This is our fight, for our time, for today. Let us practice Catholic Bushido, which is virtue. This is our way, the way of the Catholic warrior.

Scripture for Reflection

"For the flesh has desires against the Spirit, and the Spirit against the flesh; these are opposed to each other, so that you may not do what you want. But if you are guided by the Spirit, you are not under the law. Now the works of the flesh are obvious: immorality, impurity, licentiousness, idolatry, sorcery, hatreds, rivalry, jealousy, outbursts of fury, acts of selfishness, dissensions, factions, occasions of envy, drinking bouts, orgies, and the like. I warn you, as I warned you before, that those who do such things will not inherit the kingdom of God. In contrast, the fruit of the Spirit is love, joy, peace, patience, kindness, generosity, faithfulness, gentleness, self-control. Against such there is no law."

—*Galatians 5:17–23*

Wisdom of the Saints

"I do not know whether anyone has ever succeeded in not enjoying praise. And, if he enjoys it, he naturally wants to receive it. And if he wants to receive it, he cannot help but being distraught at losing it. Those who are in love with applause have their spirits starved not only when they are blamed off-hand, but even when they fail to be constantly praised."

—*St. John Chrysostom*[10]

3

Prudence

Learning and Choosing the Right Way

I remember being on a canoe trip in college with three of my friends. This was one of those canoe trips where you go to a rental place and they bus you, along with the canoes and about fifteen other people, to a location upstream, drop you off, and you float back to a prescribed pick-up location. The four of us had spent all day floating down the river, joking around, and having fun. By the time we got back, we were tired and a little fuzzy headed.

We had all pulled our canoes out of the water and were waiting for them to be loaded up when suddenly I made a split decision and started running for the river bank. I got to the edge of the water, jumped up as high as I could, and dove head first into the river. All I can remember of what happened next was a flash going off in my head and walking out of the river with everyone staring at me. I reached my hand up to rub my forehead, and it came back covered in blood. I had dived headfirst into a rock just under the water's surface and had two large gashes on my forehead.

The rest of the story is comprised of a long drive on the bus with a rag to my head, a trip to the emergency room, and stitches. In reality I am fortunate that I only needed stitches. Afterward I heard stories of people who did exactly what I had done yet ended up paralyzed. My decision that day was *not* prudent. I did not think about what could possibly happen—I just did it, and I paid the price.

The *Catechism of the Catholic Church* defines prudence as "the virtue that disposes practical reason to discern our true good in every circumstance and to choose the right means of achieving it."[1] It is the practical virtue of how we go about making decisions and then acting on them. Dilemmas both great and small occur constantly throughout our entire life:

- Should I ask Tammy to the prom (when she just broke up with my best friend)?
- Should we buy that beer?
- Should I try marijuana for the first time?

- What should I choose as a college major?
- Should I ask her to marry me?
- Who should I vote for?
- Should I accept this new job offer?
- Is now a good time to have kids?
- Our priest said something that made me angry; should I leave the parish?
- What words do I use to tell my overweight friend she needs to take better care of her health?

The need to make prudent decisions covers all aspects of your life from what you do or don't do, to what you say or don't say. You need this virtue to help you get it right.

Why Is Prudence Important and What Do I Get Out of It?

Practicing prudence helps us to steer the right course through life. Think of it like a map or a GPS system in a car. These tools help you first to find the destination you want to get to, then to decide on the correct route to follow, and finally to make all of the right turns at the correct times. This is prudence in action. You can see why it is called the charioteer of all the virtues.[2] Prudence helps to provide direction to the other virtues of fortitude, justice, and temperance.

Aside from arriving at the correct "place," we experience other benefits through practicing prudence, one of which is peace of mind. If you know that you have given your best effort to determine the right path forward in a given situation, you will have a greater sense of interior peace even when some personal sacrifice is required along the way. In the long run, you will be happier and have fewer regrets when you consistently make prudent decisions. Your relationships with others will also be stronger and more joyful since you will hurt fewer people through your words or deeds. So prudence makes you a trustworthy person. As you continue to exercise prudence, you will gain a reputation for having a thoughtful and deliberate approach to situations, and you will be able to help others in their decision-making process. Through practicing prudence, you develop wisdom.

Applying and Practicing Prudence

As I reflect on the definition presented by the Catechism and this idea of being disposed to discerning our true good, three underlying concepts come to mind:

1. In order to be disposed to discerning goodness, there must be an objective good that exists outside of myself, one not based on my feelings or emotions.

2. To exercise prudence, I must be personally motivated and inspired by love. I must be willing to set aside my own desires and feelings and potentially sacrifice something to allow the good to occur.

3. To exercise prudence, I must act honestly and develop humility by recognizing that I may not immediately "know" the right answer or what the true good is in a particular circumstance.

The person who practices prudence humbly acknowledges the good that is greater than himself; desires to know it, to do it, to be in it; and admits that he may not know exactly how to achieve the good he desires.

Part of the nature of prudence, then, is striving to *know* the true good. That good is a person, Jesus Christ. While practicing this virtue, we simultaneously work to ensure our consciences are formed based on the truth of Christ as taught by His holy church. A continuous striving to know our Lord, to grow in love for Him and for His people, is the bedrock upon which prudence functions. The more we know His truth in our hearts and minds, the more clearly we see the right path to take. So a complementary part of practicing prudence is to develop our knowledge of God's truth by studying Scripture, the writings of the saints, and the teachings of the church.

What does it mean, though, to "practice" prudence? Practice means effort. Many of us have played instruments or sports or been involved in theatre, and so we understand the need for practice. We, as created human beings, are not perfect out of the gate. This is why we practice, so that we learn to be better. How glorious that we are made this way! We study, we practice, and slowly over time we become different people. Consider it: we were made to transform, to continuously become new. Unlike the larva in the cocoon that transforms once, we are constantly changing and, by God's grace, bursting forth, becoming more of who we are meant to be in Christ, making the world a more beautiful place. This transformation happens through the practice of virtue, a lifestyle inspired and enabled by God's grace.

To truly practice prudence, then, you must work to incorporate it into your daily living. You must live consciously, "awake" to life and the situations you find yourself in. You must be aware of the multiple decisions you are making daily and apply the virtue appropriately. At the same time, take care not to become excessively scrupulous regarding mundane decisions such as how to cook your eggs this morning. In other words, you should prudently apply prudence.

Examples of Practicing Prudence

Joining a Religious Order

The details of the process differ based on the order itself; however, generally speaking, entering a religious order follows this stepwise process: First, a person expresses interest in the order, and if he appears to be a suitable candidate, he is allowed to visit and observe for several months; he then enters as a postulant and lives the community life for another period of several months; if at the end of this time both the candidate and the community are willing, he will enter the novitiate for a period of several years; he then takes first vows and then final vows. Each of these steps takes months or years.

This is an example of "institutional prudence." The sole purpose for these various lengthy steps is to allow the individual and community to deliberate and determine whether this is the right decision for each party. It must be a fit in both directions. This also highlights how patience is a central complementary attribute that enables the practice of prudence.

Deciding to Marry

We often think of a marriage proposal as the irrepressible result of an overflow of romance and love—but as a life-altering decision, this should be an exercise in prudence. The church is an ally in this regard, providing a prospective couple with a Pre-Cana process that helps them to analyze their compatibility. Prudence requires us to look at things in their true light, to see them as they really are, not necessarily how we want to see them. Prudence does its best to thwart decisions based on fleeting emotions.

Fatherhood

As a father of two sons, my work for the last twenty years has been to attempt to instill the virtue of prudence into them. This has been difficult and frustrating work at times. As I reflect on this endeavor, part of the struggle comes from the lack of experiences available for young people to draw from. At some point, young people branch out and start to make their own decisions with or without your input. The best thing you can do as a father is to find a way to ensure that your children experience the results of their decisions both good and bad (within reason) from as young an age as possible. When they break curfew, let them experience a temporary loss of privilege. When they get an A on a hard exam, let them receive a reward. When they choose not to practice and end up losing the ball game or making mistakes at the band concert, instead of telling them, "It happens," ask them, "Do you see why that happened?" Over time they will begin to develop wisdom as they understand the laws of cause and effect and the power of their actions. Armed with the memory of these experiences, in the future they will be able to think prudently through a situation and project what each response could lead to. It is our duty as fathers to strengthen our children, and we can do this by teaching them prudence.

Career and Family

In my personal life, I had a decision to make when my sons were about eight and ten. At that time, they were both involved in sports, and I was involved in coaching them. A manager at work approached me and asked if I would consider applying for a new position that had just been created. This new position would require significant travel; on average I would be away from home several days each week. As I thought through this offer (which included an increase in salary), I knew that I would have to stop coaching and that likely I would be missing several of their games. It was not a long or hard deliberation process for me. We were doing fine financially, and neither I nor my family felt the "need" for more money or things. I knew that my boys would be young only once; I would only have these years and limited opportunities to directly participate in their interests. So I declined the offer and did not pursue the job. I know this was the right decision for me and my family. I have never looked back or wished I had done differently.

Catholic Bushido

Our goal as Catholic warriors is to practice prudence and make wise decisions. We will be attacked by the emotions of frustration, anger, infatuation, lust, and depression, among others. The prudent warrior, however, knows these battles are coming and knows that he must not be led by impulse or emotion. It is not always easy to be disciplined in this way, but by prayer and reliance on God we can do it. The following 3-step process helps us to practically apply the virtue of prudence to any situation:[3]

1. **Deliberation**: Gather information. Compile what you know and consult the trusted sources available to you. It is critical that you solicit input from knowledgeable, wise, and objective sources. If you only look for input from sources that agree with your desires, then you are not practicing prudence. On matters of the spiritual life, finding a parish priest or spiritual advisor is appropriate.

2. **Judgment**: After collecting the input and information, separate relevant information from irrelevant and weigh your best options. Determine the most appropriate course of action.

3. **Execution**: Now is when you act. You have thought through the situation to the best of your ability, weighed the pros and cons, and now you must move forward and act on your decision. Remember, prudence is right reason applied to action.

Things to Consider When Practicing Prudence

1. Be prepared to have your patience tested. I am impatient and sometimes lazy—I hate waiting. I sometimes make rash decisions and would rather take my chances than think everything through. But be patient and do your best to think about the situation objectively.

2. Consider who your group of trusted advisors will be when the time comes to deliberate. Who can you go to for advice? Your spouse? A parent? An in-law? A group of friends? Your parish priest? Think about it before the moment of crisis comes. Maybe there are certain people you would go to in one type of crisis and others you would consult in a different set of circumstances.

3. When put into the position of needing to make a judgment, know and admit your limitations. Don't ever feel that you need to be an expert in an unfamiliar scenario. It is okay not to know it all.

4. Remember that at the end of deliberating and making a judgment, action must be taken. If you clearly think through a situation and determine as best as possible the right action to take—yet do not take it—then you are acting imprudently.

5. Pray the entire time! Take hope in God's direction and grace.

Prayer

O heavenly Father, we come before You as children on this earth. We are Your children. You have put into us a desire for good and for happiness. Help us to know where true happiness lies: in You and in Your Son Jesus. Lord, as we go about our lives, in the varied places and situations in which we find ourselves, give us the light of Your wisdom and be the lamp unto our feet. Help us to clearly see the path ahead that leads to You, and give us the courage and strength we need to always choose it. Amen.

Scripture for Reflection

"'I call heaven and earth today to witness against you: I have set before you life and death, the blessing and the curse. Choose life, then, that you and your descendants may live, by loving the LORD, your God, obeying his voice, and holding fast to him. For that will mean life for you, a long life for you to live on the land which the LORD swore to your ancestors, to Abraham, Isaac, and Jacob, to give to them.'"

—Deuteronomy 30:19–20

"'Which of you wishing to construct a tower does not first sit down and calculate the cost to see if there is enough for its completion? Otherwise, after laying the foundation and finding himself unable to finish the work the onlookers should laugh at him and say, "This one began to build but did not have the resources to finish."'"

—Luke 14:28–30

"I, Wisdom, dwell with prudence, and useful knowledge I have."

—Proverbs 8:12

"The fool spurns a father's instruction, but whoever heeds reproof is prudent."

—*Proverbs 15:5*

"The way of fools is right in their own eyes, but those who listen to advice are the wise."

—*Proverbs 12:15*

"In all circumstances give thanks, for this is the will of God for you in Christ Jesus. Do not quench the Spirit. Do not despise prophetic utterances. Test everything; retain what is good."

—*1 Thessalonians 5:18–21*

Wisdom of the Saints

"Blessed the one who does not speak through hope of reward, who is not always ready to unburden himself of secrets, who is not anxious to speak, but who reflects prudently on what he is to say and the manner in which he is to reply."

—*St. Francis of Assisi*[4]

"Most men seem to live according to sense rather than reason."

—*St. Thomas Aquinas*[5]

Questions for Reflection

1. Have you ever heard of anyone being called a prude? Why should this be taken as a compliment rather than a put down?
2. How is prudence related to experience? Can people be prudent when they have limited experience?
3. How does prudence relate to wisdom?
4. Why would people rather have a prudent friend or spouse rather than an impulsive one?
5. What are the three basic steps to acting prudently?

4

Justice

Who Among Us is the Just One?

"Justice was served today."

"Well, he got what was coming to him."

"She deserved it."

These quotes tend to capture our popular notion of justice, in which something negative happens to a bad actor. The main sentiment is that justice must be punitive. Justice is what people receive from a judge after the commission of a crime. Justice is the poncho-clad Clint Eastwood with his half-chewed cigar taking care of business with his Colt 45. This view of justice is one of separation, of us versus them.

But in section 1807 of the *Catechism of the Catholic Church*, justice is defined much differently:

> "Justice is the moral virtue that consists in the constant and firm will to give their due to God and neighbor. Justice toward God is called the 'virtue of religion.' Justice toward men disposes one to respect the rights of each and to establish in human relationships the harmony that promotes equity with regard to persons and to the common good. The just man, often mentioned in the Sacred Scriptures, is distinguished by habitual right thinking and the uprightness of his conduct toward his neighbor."[1]

In the Catechism's definition of justice, certain words stand out: give, respect, harmony, equity, common good, uprightness. These words describe in some way relation or interaction between persons. They are not intended to describe life in a solitary or singular existence or one based on competition. In his work *Politics*, Aristotle says, "Man is by nature a social animal; …. Anyone who either cannot lead the common life or is so self-sufficient as not to need to, and therefore does not partake of society, is either a beast or a god."[2] As human beings, we are meant to be in society, to live together, work together, build and prosper together. Even the most basic of our actions, procreation, tells us this: We cannot do it alone.

Practically speaking, then, the virtue of justice is this present reality, the place and moment in space and in time where you and I—where **we**—interact and are fair with one another. For this to happen, justice demands that we recognize "the other." We must see there is someone else just as important as we ourselves—not more, not less. The Catechism says it this way: that we recognize our brothers and sisters as "another self." When we look at others with this perspective, we see that justice is not simply a punitive decision that pits me and mine against you and yours. On the contrary, the virtue and spirit of justice brings humanity together; it brings us into harmony with one another and with God.

Another Self

In the Gospel of Matthew, Jesus says, "Gross is the heart of this people, they will hardly hear with their ears, they have closed their eyes, lest they see with their eyes and hear with their ears and understand with their heart and be converted and I heal them" (13:15). We must learn to see differently, to see our fellow man for who he is. Every single human person is God's creation, and this gives to all people (even our enemies and those we don't like) an equal dignity before God. It does not mean we are the same with respect to gifts, talents, or calling, but we are equal in our value as human beings. I personally have to work to clear the scales from my own eyes so that I can see people this way. This is not my natural way of seeing. I see other people as competition, a dummy, a threat, a source of pleasure, a nuisance, a drain on society, different. I am challenged to let go of these visions and to see my fellow man as God sees him.

Joseph Daczko

In his book *Conjecture of a Guilty Bystander*, Thomas Merton says this:

> "In Louisville, at the corner of Fourth and Walnut, in the center of the shopping district, I was suddenly overwhelmed with the realization that I loved all these people, that they were mine and I theirs, that we could not be alien to one another…. There is no way of telling people that they are all walking around shining like the sun."[3]

If I can see my fellow man walking around "shining like the sun," I will more likely want to be in harmony with him and give him his due. I need to see.

Justice Toward My Fellow Man

Stories of injustice between men are sometimes so outrageous that we cannot believe they're true. They often sound like something out of a Hollywood movie, yet these stories are constantly reported in the newspapers or on network news programs. We hear stories of corporate theft, of individuals stealing from the church treasury, of cheating and betrayal. What often goes unreported, however, are the daily stories of justice, of one person dealing fairly and openly with another. We never hear about the home remodeler who forgives the final installment owed to him by an owner unsatisfied with the results. Or about the child in sixth grade who finds a twenty-dollar bill in the school hallway and turns it into the school principal because he knows that one of his classmates must be looking for it.

61

One day I was checking out at a grocery store intending to buy, among other things, two bags of potato chips. The teenage boy who was working the register missed ringing up one of the bags and totaled my bill before I could say anything. When he gave me the total, I told him that he forgot to ring up one of the bags. This seemed to fluster him a little, and so he said, "Don't worry about it." Meaning I should just take it—he was going to give it to me for free. I looked at him and said, "Thanks but no, just keep it and restock it, please." By the look he gave me, you would have thought I had just grown a third eye. Obviously, he did not think it was any big deal to give away a bag of potato chips (and in the grander scheme of things, maybe it's not), but I thought it was obvious I should say no to something I didn't pay for. In a small way I suppose I was practicing justice with the owners of the grocery store, and they didn't even know it. Practicing justice or injustice does not require both parties to clearly know what is happening. It only requires one to know and take action.

The virtue of justice as it relates to my fellow man is most certainly central to the topic of social justice. Section 1928 of the *Catechism of the Catholic Church* says that "society ensures social justice when it provides the conditions that allow associations or individuals to obtain what is their due, according to their nature and their vocation. Social Justice is linked to the common good and the exercise of authority."[4] Social justice does not dictate who gets what and how much, but rather maintains a societal structure that promotes fairness and allows people to obtain their due. It stresses the equal dignity of every person; excessive social or economic inequalities are an affront to this dignity and can be sinful.

My Creator

The virtue of justice says that I also should give God His due. But what is God's due? What do I owe Him? The almighty God is my creator, and I am His creation. He is the infinite God, outside of space and outside of time while I, on the other hand, am finite. My relationship to God should admit and reflect this knowledge. This is the dimension of justice regarding my relationship to God: to know that we owe everything to Him, but also to know that what He really wants from us is our love. He needs nothing but wants relationship with us. "For it is loyalty that I desire, not sacrifice, and knowledge of God rather than burnt offerings" (Hosea 6:6).

Justice Toward God

In the Gospel of Luke, Jesus says to His followers, "Repay to Caesar what belongs to Caesar and to God what belongs to God" (20:25). But what do I have that God desires? How about my time? Many of us go to Mass every Sunday, and in this gesture we are already practicing justice toward God as we worship Him. We are giving God back a piece of our time. He has given us life, and in a very basic way, our time is our life. As Catholics, attending and participating in Mass is a concrete way for us to act justly. During Mass, in the prayer just before the consecration, the priest says, "Lift up your hearts," and we respond, "Let us lift them up to the Lord." The priest then says, "Let us give thanks to the Lord our God," to which we respond, "It is right and just." And it *is* right and just. It is right and just to give thanks to the Lord. God is due our worship because He is the maker and Creator of all that is, including us. He exists outside of space and outside of time. He deserves to be thanked, worshipped, and adored. We do this by being committed and attending Mass every week.

There are other ways to practice justice toward God, such as personally striving to know Him better through reading Scripture and through personal prayer. During prayer, we can spend time alone with God and allow Him to speak. Quietly waiting on Him and allowing His Spirit to be in control of some of my prayer time is just, because in this way I am putting Him first and acknowledging my position relative to Him. We are essentially putting ourselves in the position of saying, "God, I want to know what You have to say. I want to know what You want from my life."

We can also foster within ourselves a spirit of daily gratitude. As we go through our busy days that are normally jammed full of activities, let's make it a practice to regularly pause, even for twenty seconds at a time, and be grateful. Let's be grateful for the new day as we drive to work. For the shining sun on the first days of spring. Let's be grateful for our families and friends as we spend time with and think about them. Let's be grateful as we eat our three meals a day, actually saying grace as a family when eating out at a restaurant. Let's be grateful for our homes, beds, clothes, for a hot shower and a cold drink of water. Let's be grateful for our childhood memories and for the potential that today brings. Let's be grateful for all things. In practicing justice this way, you will know God better and see Him in all things while at the same time affecting a positive transformation in your general outlook on life.

Justice in My Family

As parents, Angela and I have always tried to act justly with our boys. We have tried to be fair and equitable in our expectations of their behavior with respect to the chores we would assign them, with the type and severity of our discipline, even in the quantity and types of gifts we would get them for Christmas. I do not mean that we would treat them identically, only that we would treat them fairly. We have also tried to teach them that the reason why they have responsibilities around the home is not because we say so (although we certainly do), but because they are a part of the family—and so our home and everything in it is also theirs to care for. It's not easy trying to instill this understanding in a child. Truthfully, I am not sure we can instill it at all. At best, we plant the seeds, nurture them, and hope they blossom in time. Here the concept of justice means "we are all in this together." It's us, everyone.

My wife has been instrumental in showing me another way of practicing justice in our family. This centers on giving others the chance to speak and express their opinion. I have historically been a "football coach" of a dad: I say—you do. To a certain extent, this is needed and okay as it creates a sense of discipline and respect. However, it must be balanced to ensure "the other" is being respected. As my boys have grown older, Angela has helped me to see that I need to grow and mature with them as a father—specifically, I need to get better at listening to them. Listening does not necessarily mean changing my position, but rather hearing what they have to say, prudently reflecting on their words, and then deciding whether I need to adjust my way of thinking. This doesn't feel like second nature yet, but I'll keep working at it. I must remember that I am practicing justice with my boys when I allow them to share contrary opinions and sincerely listen.

So practicing justice with my fellow man can be as simple as not taking an unpaid-for bag of chips, or it can entail honestly working through multi-million-dollar business deals. Justice does not always revolve around money or actions; merely allowing others to talk and give their point of view can be a gift of justice. This can be practiced in the family, in church, at work or in larger social settings. One way for us to promote justice in this regard would be to help those less fortunate, or those on the margins of society to have a voice in the public forum. Help to ensure that the lowly ones' needs and voices are being heard along with everyone else.

Justice and Law

The virtue of justice is what serves as the deep foundation for our human justice system—this virtue informs our laws. Laws should flow from the true knowledge of what is just. If we take the opposite perspective, supposing that any act permitted by law is just, we'd live our lives in search of every last loophole. Some people do exactly that, flaunting justice. When we see evil go unpunished, it offends our conscience. But we cannot restore justice through better or broader laws. Virtue cannot be legislated, because virtue is in the spirit and heart of each individual. A law cannot make someone be different; it can only set limitations on actions. The Catechism says that the just man is distinguished not only by the uprightness of his conduct toward his neighbor but by upright thinking. We cannot hope to turn hearts and minds to justice through force of law, but if we faithfully practice justice ourselves, we can have an impact.

Catholic Bushido

We are called as men to have the right view of ourselves in relation to our neighbor and to God. Justice is about how we relate to each other and get along together. We are not more important than any other human being, nor are we less important. We are called to protect and promote our own sense of dignity and the dignity of our neighbors in a world that often seems cruel and uncaring. We protect and promote dignity first and foremost by how we interact with other men. By seeing and treating them as another self.

We are also called and expected to practice justice relative to God our Father. God has created us, and He does not ask for much, except that we love Him and desire to share relationship with Him. Strive to do this; strive to instill this perspective in your families. We do owe God everything. He is the foundation of our very existence.

Justice is not a punitive action intended to separate or expel. It is the way of being that governs how we interact as the human family in relation to one another and to God. When practiced by all, justice brings togetherness and harmony.

Prayer

Lord God, Father of all, give me a greater desire to know You, to recognize You for who You are. Let me clearly see my right relationship to You: I, a finite creation, loved by my infinite Creator. May my love for You grow and bring me to the place where worshipping You is my whole joy. Lord, may I be transformed this way, and may this love for You flow from me as I interact with my fellow man. May I see him as You see him, as one shining like the sun. May I see him as my equal and ensure he receives his due. In Your name, I pray. Amen.

Scripture for Reflection

"The evil understand nothing of justice, but those who seek the LORD understand everything."

—*Proverbs 28:5*

"Learn to do good. Make justice your aim: redress the wronged, hear the orphan's plea, defend the widow."

—*Isaiah 1:17*

"You shall not act dishonestly in rendering judgment. Show neither partiality to the weak nor deference to the mighty but judge your neighbor justly."

—*Leviticus 19:15*

"So he said to them, 'Then repay to Caesar what belongs to Caesar and to God what belongs to God.'"

—*Luke 20:25*

"Thus says the LORD of hosts: Judge with true justice and show kindness and compassion toward each other."

—*Zechariah 7:9*

"You have been told, O mortal, what is good, and what the LORD requires of you: Only to do justice and to love goodness, and to walk humbly with your God."

—*Micah 6:8*

Wisdom of the Saints

"Blessed is the servant who esteems himself no better when he is praised and exalted by people than when he is considered worthless, simple, and despicable; for what a man is before God, that he is and nothing more."

—*St. Francis of Assisi*[5]

"Mercy without justice is the mother of dissolution; justice without mercy is cruelty."

—*St. Thomas Aquinas*[6]

"By nature all men are equal in liberty, but not in other endowments."

—*St. Thomas Aquinas*[7]

"If we have no peace, it is because we have forgotten that we belong to each other."

—*St. Teresa of Calcutta*[8]

Questions for Reflection

1. How would you explain the church's definition of justice?

2. Is justice about protecting what's yours? If not, what is it about?

3. How is justice toward God and justice toward men related?

4. How do we practice justice in our relationships?

5. Can we pass a law that would guarantee justice in every situation?

5

Temperance

The Animal Trainer

M y father trained as a civil engineer and worked as the president of a marine construction company for decades. His company had offices and conducted work in the U.S. and Canada, but also throughout Latin America, Japan, Hong Kong, and many other locations around the world. He had many business associates, and when they were in town my father would bring them to our house, sometimes for dinner, sometimes just to relax. As I grew up, I was fortunate to be exposed to different kinds of people from many places around the world. One gentleman from South America visited us many times; he and his family became friends with my father and our family. My dad once told me a story about an interaction I had with this man when I was very young (too young for me to have my own memories of the event). This man and I were talking—the topic of our conversation remains a mystery—but as we finished, the man looked up at my mother, pointed at me, and said, "This one here...he is always trying to get candy."

I remember that story not because of its earth-shaking impact on my life, but rather because a near-stranger from South America saw into my adolescent soul. He was right. When I was little, candy was it. If there was candy anywhere in the house—"Game on"—I was on the prowl. I was always in search of candy, and when I found it I would not share it with anyone. At Christmas time, my mother liked to make M&M cookies, but she would have to hide the M&M candies or else I would find them and eat them before she could do her baking. Unfortunately for her, I came to know where all of her hiding places were.

Here are the depths to which I would go to score the best candy: I am the youngest of five children, and one Easter morning I got out of bed before my brothers and sisters and went in search of everyone's Easter baskets. I found them and took all of the good stuff from my brothers' and sisters' baskets and put it in mine. I was shameless in my continuing quest for candy. Yes, I was young, but even for my age I had a remarkable lack of self-restraint. I was determined to satisfy my passion for candy regardless of whose Easter basket I had to violate. I needed to learn to practice the virtue of temperance.

In paragraph 1809, the *Catechism of the Catholic Church* defines temperance as "the moral virtue that moderates the attraction of pleasures and provides balance in the use of created goods. It ensures the will's mastery over instincts and keeps desires within the limits of what is honorable. The temperate person directs the sensitive appetites toward what is good and maintains a healthy discretion."[1]

So, balance is the word. In practicing temperance, we recognize the good things in the world for what they are, develop the will necessary to keep our desires for these good things in check, and limit our efforts to acquire our fill of them.

Why Practice Temperance?

Temperance is like an animal trainer. Think of the lion tamer at the circus or even the local owner of a dog obedience school. Animals want to act instinctively; they want to react and go, move, do in the moment. The lion tamer is there to ensure the lions do not follow their immediate instincts but do as commanded.

Let's not kid ourselves, our desires for pleasure and comfort are very strong. Without us knowing, they can direct and control both our thoughts and actions. For example, alcoholics, drug addicts, the grossly obese, and pornography addicts are not practicing temperance. They are driven to use things to the extreme. If you fail to exercise temperance, over time these compulsive desires will begin to dominate your thoughts; before you know it, your mental, emotional, and physical freedom will become compromised. You will no longer be able to make decisions or choices freely as these dominating desires start to color and influence each choice you make. Finally, you will become completely swallowed up and trapped inside a box of your own desires. Desires that do not satisfy. And you'll be lost.

Once I am consumed by my own desires, I no longer have room for "another self," and this can cause division. Consider this scenario: You are at a wedding reception waiting for your table to be summoned to the buffet. You have been waiting for a piece of fried chicken (since fried chicken always seems to be on a wedding buffet menu) since you first arrived at the reception hall. Sitting at your table is a young man that has also been waiting. You two have been talking about fried chicken for the last thirty minutes. Your table is finally called, and he gets in line just in front of you. Looking ahead, you see that there are about four pieces of chicken left in the pan. The young man approaches and takes all four, leaving you none. You are in a state of disbelief—he knew you were waiting in anticipation to have chicken too. How could he take it all? His lack of temperance has emotionally impacted you. It has caused a certain "separation" to come between you. You both make your way back to your table, he with his four pieces of chicken and you with none. How does your conversation go for the rest of the evening? Had he been practicing temperance, he would have been more disposed to thinking of you as his brother and would not have missed the opportunity to draw the two of you together in solidarity.

In further considering the importance of temperance, I would ask a question. What is the purpose of your existence? Are you here on this earth by chance? Is there any reason you shouldn't try to have as much fun, pleasure, good feelings, and entertainment as possible? Is your life all about you? In today's society, some would absolutely agree: this is all there is to life, you deserve it all, go get it. But I wholeheartedly disagree with this sentiment. I don't pretend to know your life purpose or God's mission for you, but I know we are all here for a reason. **I know that your life and my life matter**. Pope Benedict XVI said, "The world promises you comfort, but you were not made for comfort, you were made for greatness."[2] Our lives are about something much bigger than comfort and pleasure. We are meant to rise above our natural instincts and desires—to control them—and be transformed into children of God. As children of God, we will treat one another with greater consideration and kindness. We will willfully love one another. This is our hope and our call.

Practicing temperance therefore puts the Catholic warrior's will in command of his desires and frees him from their tornado of bondage. We practice this virtue so that we can grow in our freedom to choose to love our brother and our God. No one can serve both God and mammon (Matthew 6:24), and it is only in God that our true self exists and can be found. The practice of temperance defends this freedom—to ultimately become who we are meant to be in Him.

For many years, I lived a life completely absorbed by my own physical wants and desires. I have experienced in my own life the painful and tragic results of selfish living, having hurt myself and other people terribly. My personal knowledge of this place of isolation and sadness informs my confidence that there is more to life than my own enjoyment and pleasure. Worldly things do not satisfy. I know there is something better to live for, and I hope that you trust me when I say this. My desire to practice temperance flows from this personal knowledge and from the belief that our loving God has made each and every one of us for a reason. If we simply strive to satisfy our natural desires, we'll never be truly fulfilled. Pursue your true purpose instead. It may feel like a mystery, but God will faithfully lead you. Walking in His light will bring you your greatest joy.

How Do We Practice Temperance?

As anyone who really knows me can attest, my favorite spiritual teacher and writer is Thomas Merton. Merton was a Trappist monk who lived, taught, and wrote at the Abbey of Gethsemani near Bardstown, Kentucky. I was first introduced to his works when I was in my mid-twenties. My wife and I were just starting our journey back into the church. At one of our church meetings, a parishioner by the name of Lillian Kryzanski showed a video dramatization of the story of Thomas Merton. The man onscreen was just an actor, but I couldn't take my eyes off the screen as he read one of Merton's works. I have been fascinated by Merton ever since, and I have read and listened to his words regularly.

What intrigued me from the very beginning with Thomas Merton was the life that he came from prior to becoming Catholic. He was a very worldly man in all senses of the word. But he was transformed. Through his conversion, faith, and relationship with Christ, he became a new man with many gifts to share. Ultimately, as I proceeded to read more of his work, two things really struck my heart: the concept of silence—especially the peace associated with silently sitting before God and hearing what He has to say—and his description of the profundity of a personal and contemplative relationship with God. In many cases I was able to grasp some of the deep wisdom that he was sharing. So the peace and the depth of understanding I received from reading his books about Jesus, prayer, and faith changed me.

Through those years of listening and learning about monastic ascetic spirituality, I learned of the concepts of renunciation and detachment. To renounce something means to take the action of rejecting it. In the monastic life, monks renounce material goods, marriage and sexual relations, and a self-directed life. This occurs through the monks' vows of poverty, chastity, and obedience. On the outside, this may look almost tragic for these men to be denied so many good things. But actually renunciation is not negative, nor is it practiced for its own merit. Monks engage in this practice to develop a spirit of detachment from worldly things. When you are detached (or not controlled by) things, you are free. Free to be a true disciple of Christ.

We may not feel called to this monastic life of intentional renunciation, but this doesn't excuse us from practicing temperance. It only means we'll have different obstacles and temptations along the way. And so our mental outlook as we start down this path is important. The mental starting point for practicing temperance is the joyful realization that God's creation is good. Many of the things I'd like to possess are good; the desire for sexual relations within the sacrament of marriage is good; my natural urge to eat and drink is good; my ability to enjoy all these is good. The key to practicing temperance is not to paint all these things as sinful, as a corruptive influence to cast aside. God Himself called His creation good, so we should not contradict Him. We must view God's creation for what it is while recognizing that there is a higher order of good that we should desire even more: relationship with God. I believe that part of our struggle is that "we want it all"—we don't want to miss anything, and so we have this drive to get as much as we can.[3] I wonder if this is a symptom of our fall in the Garden of Eden and original sin, where our first parents were tricked into thinking that they could be like gods. We reach for the *infinite*, but we cannot attain it and our *finite* lives become frustrated. We *are* finite beings, however, with only so much time and ability at our disposal. We have to learn to let go of one thing in order to have something else of greater value.

By the wisdom of the church, we have an opportunity to practice renunciation each year during the penitential season of Lent. Most of us have been programmed to just "give something up" for Lent. And in most cases, this means we stop eating chocolate, desserts, sweets, or snacks, or stop drinking beer or soda. What many of us don't grasp is that the purpose of this annual renunciation is to do penance *and* to help us develop interior freedom.

At one time I was a member of Facebook. I was surrounded by my "friends" and my news feeds. What I eventually noticed was that my pattern in the evening was to sit down at home in the evening and, rather than opening a regular book, open up Facebook. It became a time drain. I would even use it intentionally as a way to waste time rather than "do" something else. Looking back on it, Facebook was a tool that I gave to the vice of sloth to use in my life. It was keeping me from using my time effectively. So one Lent I decided to give up participating on Facebook. The experience was so amazing that I decided to make the change permanent. I have never gone back. Since that time, I have read more, learned more, and finally started writing this book. In other words, I traded away one thing and got back much more in return.

The practice of renouncing or giving things up builds into us the experience we need to practice the virtue of temperance. It gives us the critical tool necessary for success: the ability to say no to things. One way then that you can start practicing temperance is to participate in the Lenten journey. Say no to something you want, renounce your own distracting "thing." But prior to the start of Lent, give some real thought to what the object of your renunciation should be. Then when the season of Lent arrives, participate fully: fast, observe the days of abstinence from meat, pray more, and give alms. Lent is a training ground for temperance, so take advantage of it. But at the same time, maintain proper motives. See Lent for what it is: a time for us to show Jesus how much we love Him. We "give things up" to do penance and demonstrate sorrow for our failings, but also to be cleansed and drawn into closer relationship with Jesus who is our life.

We should also take steps of *joyful renunciation* outside of the time of Lent. We can make small sacrifices daily or weekly. Just do it at regular intervals. Plan it out as if you were setting up a physical training schedule. I know that I need to make these sacrifices regularly to stay in practice; then I will be ready when the real temptations come and my abilities to say no are tested. I believe that once I faithfully put my feet onto this path, God will lead me to the areas in my life where temperance is most needed.

Only God Knows

In many ways, practicing temperance is very personal. As long as a person is maintaining his practice of temperance, we won't be able to determine what is happening in his spirit or what his true needs are. Harmful desires put into action, on the other hand, are easy to spot. These destructive behaviors should prompt us to come to the aid of our struggling friend or family member and help him back to the path of temperance.

Our transformational path to sanctity takes a lifetime, and your path is yours alone. Only God knows the full truth of who and what each of us really are. We don't even know the full truth ourselves. If I don't know the total truth about myself, how can I know anything about your soul? What we must do is support one another in the steps we each take alone towards sanctity. This is not to say that everyone can go along their own way in any direction and still be on the "right" path. There is objective truth which we must strive to know. However, we are not all identical in what we must do or in what our spiritual needs are. And we could all use a little encouragement once in a while. Let's help our brothers walk their path.

Joseph Daczko

Examples of Practicing Temperance

My Marriage

My wife and I had our first child, Nate, in 1998. I'll never forget the day he was born. I was there in the delivery room the entire time. Angi was pushing and working, and finally I could see the top of this little head. Then, just like that, this little human baby came slipping out. One moment all that was visible was the top of a wet, hairy head, and in the next, a complete baby boy. It was amazing. We were so happy—but then Angi started experiencing severe pain and discomfort. There I was, holding my newborn son with a half-smile on my face only to see Angi's doctor with a very serious look on hers. I did not know what to think. It turned out she was suffering from HELLP syndrome, a life-threatening complication that can strike immediately after childbirth. Her liver was swelling, her organs were failing, and she was bleeding out. She easily could have died. She even received the sacrament of last rites. If we were not in a hospital, she likely would not have survived.

Needless to say, this experience during the birth of our first son stuck with us and scared us. We were both frightened at the thought of her getting pregnant again. We had been back in the church and seriously practicing our faith at this point and knew that artificial contraception was not an option for us. We lived through some times of struggle and frustration, and then my wife ended up learning about Natural Family Planning (NFP). Initially, I was not very excited about this program, and I struggled with it. The struggle occurred during the times when Angi was fertile; during these times we were required to completely abstain from sexual relations. This amounted to anywhere from 50–65% of the time. I am very attracted to my wife, so this never got "easy," but we maintained our discipline. Practicing temperance does not promise to be easy at first, and it may never become easy—like love, it is a willful choice. Sometimes it was my wife's will that pulled us through, and sometimes mine was strong enough. Either way, we practiced temperance together.

Parish Men's Faith Group

Before our first son was born, when my wife and I were becoming more and more active in our parish, we formed a prayer and Bible study group with two other couples. This group continued to meet for over twenty years. During these years, many different people and couples came through to study and pray with us. We studied apologetics, the Eucharist, the fathers of the church, the virtues, the charismatic gifts, icons, the Trinity—the list could go on and on. This prayer group was created and led by God through the Holy Spirit. Today we all take part in various parish ministries as God leads us, and we are all still very good friends.

I am currently involved in our parish men's group, and within this context I can practice the virtue of temperance with my words. I have found that at certain times I will tend to speak up with my thoughts and ideas rather than letting someone else fill the silent pauses. I want to speak and share with these men, but God has shown me that He wants other men to stand up and speak. He wants them to become leaders and strong, prayerful men who are willing *and* able to verbalize their faith and explain it in some detail. One way I can help this happen is by giving them room to develop during our men's group meetings. God has asked me to hold back, stay quiet, and practice temperance in a subtler but no less important way. My practice of temperance will benefit these men who are now starting their journey. It will give them the freedom to develop and become more Christlike.

Catholic Bushido

Practicing temperance will at first be uncomfortable. It may be a small nuisance. But if the thing we are trying to rein in is big and buried deep inside of us, we may be in for a serious and prolonged struggle. In these moments, remember the slogan "no pain, no gain." These painful and lonely times in the spiritual life can bring much growth and grace. The thing to remember is that it can be done: others have come and gone before us fighting the same struggle, failing, standing back up, failing again, moving forward, continuing, never giving up.

Men, as Catholic warriors, you must not give up. Allow me to quote my inner Winston Churchill:

> "Together, Catholic brothers, looking straight into the face of our own internal spiritual tyranny, using the virtues, we will fight in our homes, we will fight in our parishes and in our schools, we will fight in our places of work, we will fight in our places of recreation, in the shopping malls, in our cars, while walking to work. In order to change the world, starting in our own shoes we will resist the evil one through all the

tools our Lord and our church have provided. We may fail, but we will rise again to fight anew; we will never surrender."

Prayer

My Lord God, You have created all things, and all of Your creation is good. Help us to see the created world through Your eyes, to see its beauty, to experience its goodness, but at the same time to have freedom from it. Help us to always choose the highest good, the good that leads to union with You, the good that fulfills our being because it is Your design for us. May we, in our heart of hearts, want that more than anything, and may we have the fortitude to fight for it always without surrender. Amen.

Scripture for Reflection

"If you find honey, eat only what you need, lest you have your fill and vomit it up."

—Proverbs 25:16

"Jesus answered them, 'Amen, amen, I say to you, everyone who commits sin is a slave of sin.'"

—John 8:34

"Now those who belong to Christ [Jesus] have crucified their flesh with its passions and desires."

—Galatians 5:24

"Every athlete exercises discipline in every way. They do it to win a perishable crown, but we an imperishable one. Thus I do not run aimlessly; I do not fight as if I were shadowboxing. No, I drive my body and train it, for fear that, after having preached to others, I myself should be disqualified."

—1 Corinthians 9:25–27

"For the grace of God has appeared, saving all and training us to reject godless ways and worldly desires and to live temperately, justly, and devoutly in this age, as we await the blessed hope, the appearance of the glory of the great God and of our savior Jesus Christ, who gave himself for us to deliver us from all lawlessness and to cleanse for himself a people as his own, eager to do what is good."

—Titus 2:11–14

"For freedom Christ set us free; so stand firm and do not submit again to the yoke of slavery."

—Galatians 5:1

Wisdom of the Saints

"Temperance is simply a disposition of the mind which set bounds to the passions."

—*St. Thomas Aquinas*[4]

"Not everything that is more difficult is more meritorious."

—*St. Thomas Aquinas*[5]

"Let the mouth also fast from disgraceful speeches and railings. For what does it profit if we abstain from fish and fowl and yet bite and devour our brothers and sisters? The evil speaker eats the flesh of his brother and bites the body of his neighbor."

—*St. John Chrysostom*[6]

Questions for Reflection

1. What is the relationship between the words temperature and temperance? How does this relate to our spiritual lives?

2. How is temperance related to spiritual freedom?

3. Why is spiritual freedom important?

4. How is temperance related to prudence and justice?

5. What are the various ways that you can practice temperance in your life?

6

Fortitude

Rising Again After We Fall

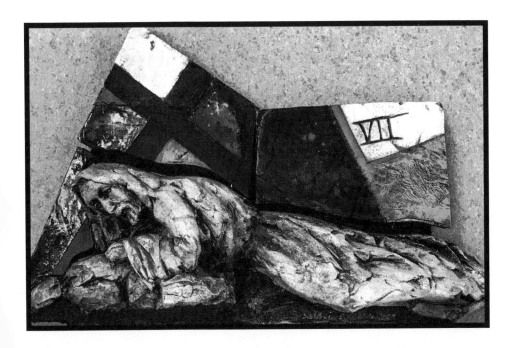

"'Father if you are willing, take this cup from me: still not my will but yours be done....' He was in such agony and prayed so fervently that his sweat became likes drops of blood falling to the ground."

—*Luke 22:42, 44*

Why was Jesus sweating and in such agony? He was afraid. Not out of weakness but out of necessity. We believe that our Lord was fully God and fully man and that He redeemed *all* of our humanity. Except for sin, everything that we experience—everything that we feel, think, and struggle with—was experienced and redeemed by Christ. The fullness of both Jesus' humanity and divinity is on display with such clarity in this part of Luke's Gospel. We see extreme human fear and divine love without reserve. Jesus the man was afraid, but as God, His love gave Him the purpose and the ability to overcome His fear and do what needed to be done. He did not turn away from the trial—He went forward into it. Fear and anxiety are a part of everyone's life. When it strikes, it can seem that we're trapped in a place with no escape. This is not true, however; there is a place through and beyond our fear. Sometimes we just need some help to get there. Jesus Christ can show us the way. The way to greater fortitude.

In paragraph 1808, the *Catechism of the Catholic Church* defines fortitude as "the moral virtue that ensures firmness in difficulties and constancy in the pursuit of the good. It strengthens the resolve to resist temptations and to overcome obstacles to the moral life. The virtue of fortitude enables one to conquer fear, even fear of death, and to face trials and persecutions."[1] Some important words I pull from this definition are firmness, strengthen, resist, overcome, conquer, and face. Two images come to mind: the first is a lighthouse with strong waves breaking against it, while the second is of a fireman running into a burning building to save those trapped inside. But Christ's agony in the garden gives us the ultimate example of fortitude.

Why is Fortitude Necessary?

Overcoming Selfishness

We all have a tendency towards selfishness; that is a fact. The church calls this *concupiscence*, or "any intense form of human desire."[2] We like to believe that we grow out of our total self-absorption, but do we really? Right out of the womb as infants, we cry when in need, but then as we grow older we learn that we can cry to get what we *want*. As we move into adulthood, we change and mature, but often the selfish part of our personality remains. It may not be as outwardly evident as it is in a crying child, but it's still there. Fortitude is the virtue that strengthens our resolve to ignore our desires and move past them, making us free to work for some good greater than our own.

Facing Fear

Fear is a strong emotion. From a historical human development standpoint, fear is a good thing. When in the wild, fear of lions, bears, or other large carnivorous beasts is healthy and promotes a longer life and continuation of the species. However, with respect to our spiritual development, and simply as persons who live together in society, fear is often a hurdle inhibiting us from traveling on our path to sanctity. But what is it that we are afraid of? This is a question we should ask ourselves. Take time with it and be completely honest.

As men in America, we are not supposed to be afraid of anything, but we should let go of this misconception. It's the ability to move forward despite our fears that makes us heroes and allows us to live the life God has called us to. According to Jaimal Yogis in his book *The Fear Project*, some of the things we fear the most are loss of security, death, stage fright, and not being liked.[3] Consider your own attitude toward security. Do you fear losing your income, your livelihood, or even your marriage and family relationships? Or do you fear losing the respect of your wife, children, or friends? If you are afraid of not being respected, it is highly likely that this fear will influence your relationships and your way of interacting with those people. Fear may keep you from being as open and as honest with them as you could be, to their detriment. Also consider the fear of "stage fright." Are you afraid of *genuinely* putting yourself out there and standing out in the crowd? Are you afraid to let people see who you really are? You shouldn't be. Fear keeps you trapped inside of yourself and places limits on the good impact you can have on the world.

Scripture tells us more than three hundred times to "fear not." For instance, when an angel appears to Mary to announce the miraculous pregnancies at hand for her and her cousin, Mary is so shaken that the angel has to tell her not to fear. Keep this in mind: when truth is revealed to us, our hearts may be troubled—even if the content of the revelation is good—because we are forced to admit that certain assumptions we had about God or the world or ourselves were false. Something in our worldview or lifestyle is going to have to change. Out of fear, we may hesitate to walk the new path God has for us. But if we practice the virtue of fortitude and take small, courageous steps forward, we will be transformed by the grace of God at work in us, becoming a new creation.

When we practice fortitude in this way, not only do we change as we realign with God's revealed truth, but we become stronger and more courageous for having faced our fear. Have you ever known an awkward and shy teenager who leaves home and goes away to school or work? When you see that individual a few years later, the difference is often striking. He is now relaxed and cordial, ready to engage in pleasant conversation. This young person has transformed and blossomed by going through potentially fearful struggles alone and coming out the other end more confident and alive. This process continues our whole lives if we let it. Run toward the struggle, not away from it.

Strengthening One Another

This virtue is also crucial to the building up of families, communities, and society as a whole. Think of the impact it has on others when they see or hear of someone performing an act of bravery. Think of the recovering addict who never uses or has a drink again for the rest of his life. Think about the convicted criminal who returns to society, gets a good job, supports his family, and refuses to fall back into his old ways. Think of the soldier running into battle, the policemen responding to an emergency call. Think of the firemen and paramedics who ran *Into* the towers on 9/11. When everyone else is running away, courageous men run directly into the fearsome situation. When we see these types of examples, our spirits are affected. The virtue of fortitude is contagious because deep inside we all personally know fear, and when we see another person overcome a fearsome situation, we are given hope. We see with *proof* that fear can be overcome. We feel this inspiration in our own spirit, accompanied by joy and renewed confidence. This confidence can change a family, a community, and a society.

Examples of Fortitude

A Little Boy

When I was a young boy, my brothers and sisters would tell stories of a "ghost" that they claimed to regularly see in our home basement. I believed their stories were true. Now, older brothers and sisters trying to scare their younger siblings is not something new. But their tales were especially traumatizing to me given the spiritual environment in our home at that time. We were in the midst of a faith detour. I was too young to know exactly how it happened or why, but a number of new-age thoughts and practices had crept in and were practiced in our home (eventually this would change with my family coming back to Christ). Words cannot do justice to the multiple emotions I felt at that time, but I can tell you that I was afraid. Something inside of me was repulsed and frightened and wanted no part of the ghost stories, seances, and other practices going on in our home. This fear seemed to be with me constantly no matter where I went in the house. Whenever I would go from one floor to the next, especially from our basement, I would run up the stairs as fast as I could. In my mind it felt like something was coming behind me, similar to that dream where something is chasing you and you try to get away but can't. The only difference is that I was awake, not asleep.

As I got a little older, I started to think about this specific fear of mine, and I remember clearly the day it changed. I was getting ready to go up the stairs from our basement to the first floor. My habit had always been to take two or three stairs at a time and to get up them as fast as I could. However, this time I walked, slowly, step by step, and stopped halfway up the stairs. I just stood there. I refused to run. The fear that had always driven me and chased me up the stairs washed over me completely. **And nothing happened**. By some grace of God, I had stood and faced this irrational fear, alone. The only people I have ever told this story to are my wife and my sons. I share it now because I believe people need to know that whether your fear is real or imagined, whether you are young or old, it can affect you. But you should also know that whatever fear you have, by God's grace, it can be overcome. I know the firmness of will I felt as I stood unmoving on those stairs decades ago, and I know that it was God giving me a taste of fortitude.

Not Giving Up on a Dream

I love the game of football. I grew up playing it on the playground, in my backyard, and ultimately for organized teams. The sport taught me many life lessons, including the importance of sacrificing for the team. Like most kids, I dreamt of being the star offensive player who scored touchdowns and made spectacular diving catches. My hero was Paul Warfield, the Hall of Fame wide receiver who played for both the Cleveland Browns and Miami Dolphins. I remember watching him in the seventies and can still see in my mind's eye a catch he made in the middle of three defenders. That's who I wanted to be and what I wanted to do. But it was not to be. I became an offensive guard, and that position followed me through my high school career. On defense, however, I learned to play defensive back and fell in love with it. I was even fortunate enough to play that position for a couple of years in a Division III college program.

The exploits of an amateur athlete may seem insignificant in the context of spiritual warfare between virtue and vice, but the lessons we learn as children play out again with higher stakes in adulthood. The point here isn't that I played one position or another but that I did not quit when my initial "dream" or expectation fell through. This is another facet of fortitude. At the time, not earning the position I really wanted was disappointing, but I continued on. I then changed focus and concentrated on being the best defensive back I could be. And so a new opportunity and hope sprouted.

From my adolescent perspective, I wasn't thinking about the virtue of fortitude; I just wanted to play football. But the virtue growing within me kept me from quitting, giving half-effort, or complaining about the coaches. I continued on, adjusted, and had a very fulfilling experience as a young man. It was probably the best thing I had going on at that point in my life.

Tom Catena

Dr. Tom Catena is the only doctor at Mother of Mercy Hospital in Africa's Nuba Mountains.[4] His hospital is on the border between Sudan and South

Sudan, and he regularly sees the results of the violent conflict that has engulfed this area for years. It is one thing to see images of broken buildings and shattered towns, but Dr. Catena knows the names and faces of those affected. Sometimes he sees small children with full-depth burns on over 60% of their body. Sometimes he sees elderly people or expectant mothers or fathers with a sick child who have no other means to receive the routine care they require. For all of these and more, he is there. He has committed himself to helping these people.

Consider what it would be like to be the only doctor in a hospital treating up to five hundred patients a day. Perhaps the patient you are now seeing needs an operation that you have never performed. What do you do? Do you give up? No. You study, you learn, you perform the surgery, and you do the best you can to try to help him recover. This is Dr. Tom Catena. He was trained in the United States as a family practitioner, yet he treats all of the patients in his hospital. Fortitude allowed him to give up his comfortable life in the United States for life in a hospital surrounded by armed conflict, it helps him carry on in that dangerous environment, and it gives him the courage to stretch himself and his skills outside of his comfort zone in order to help as many people as he can. He's not afraid to try.

Parents Need Fortitude

As parents, my wife and I have always tried to instill into our two sons the tenets of our faith. We have also tried to impress upon them the truth that our faith must be lived out through our actions. One of the societal fights we have discussed in our family is the fight for the unborn. In combination with this, we have talked about pre-marital sex, contraception, and the true purpose of sex and love. As we would talk about these things, it was always evident that the words we spoke could only really "say" so much. Our young boys had little experience that they could reflect on and connect to the truth we were telling them. So my wife and I felt we had to do something to make the faith real to all of us. We decided to go out as a family and stand in front of a Planned Parenthood abortion clinic and pray. We ended up doing this a few times. Let me assure you: if you've ever wanted to test your fortitude, try standing on a busy road with just yourself, your wife, and two small boys of about 9 and 11 years of age, pro-life signs in hand. In such a moment, you are taking a clear public stand with *nowhere* to hide. I simply pray that our time in front of the abortion clinic affected people in a positive way for Jesus and challenged their attitudes toward the unborn. I also pray that a bit of God's grace was instilled into my sons for them to remember, that they may have fortitude when their time comes.

Saint Maximilian Kolbe

St. Maximilian Kolbe was a Franciscan friar in Poland. He was imprisoned in the Auschwitz death camp during the Second World War. While he was there, a fellow prisoner, who had a wife and family, was sentenced to death. Fr. Kolbe stepped forward and offered to take the man's place. The prison camp officials accepted his offer, and St. Maximilian Kolbe was martyred.[5] This is a demonstration of fortitude and courage at the highest level.

Joseph Daczko

Most of us will never have to choose whether to put our lives on the line in such courageous and heroic fashion—but we shouldn't dismiss the importance of the dilemmas we do encounter. Just like my childhood football experience gave me an early lesson in fortitude that I can apply in weightier circumstances, every career choice and family decision is a valuable opportunity to courageously choose to follow the promptings of the Holy Spirit. As you grow in faith and courage, expect to be surprised by the places He leads you.

The men and women who join the military or the police force or the fire department do so through fortitude. Teachers do not expect to become millionaires by teaching, but they choose to make a difference in young people's lives. The young college student who chooses to focus on his studies rather than go have fun with his friends is exercising fortitude. People who contribute time to churches or civic groups do not expect to receive a personal benefit in return. Our ability to choose for the greater good impacts us all.

There are many other stories of courage and fortitude in Scripture and in our faith history. We should take some time to consider these. For example, Shadrach, Meshach, and Abednego did not bow to King Nebuchadnezzar's will and worship him, even though they knew they would be condemned to death in the white-hot furnace. In the Book of Daniel, Suzanna refuses to have sexual relations with the two elders, is falsely accused by them, stands trial, and is ultimately vindicated. Paul endured imprisonment, the Apostles emerged from their place of hiding in the upper room on the day of Pentecost, and our Blessed Mother Mary sat at the foot of the cross and watched her son die. The blood of the martyrs both historical and contemporary shouts fortitude. Our history, our foundation, is one of courage and fortitude. It manifests itself in our ability to resist our own temptations, to resist the demands placed on us by others, and to engages in proactive outward movement to stand up and speak for the truth. Fortitude is central to who we are, and we should never forget that.

How to Practice Fortitude?

Fortitude does not always require the ultimate sacrifice; like all virtues, it exists on a continuum, enabling acts that require a little bit of courage as well as those that require superhuman, divinely graced courage. So the first step in practicing fortitude is not to compare yourself to another person. You can certainly look at the actions of others to learn from them (especially the saints), but do not compare yourself. The practice of virtue is not a competition. As a matter of fact, if your goal is to prove yourself courageous, rather than to practice virtue for God's sake, you may be led to engage in extreme acts. This is recklessness, not fortitude, and is not virtuous.

Remember that the virtues are held aloft by the church for the good of both the individual and the community. The virtues invite us to protect, cherish, and honor both. In contrast, society glamorizes the "individual" above all else with stories of those who push past and through anything that stands in their way. We should remember that the "ends" never justify the "means." Meaning that although a personal success may be a good thing, it also matters "how" that success was achieved. Take, for example, a young man who becomes a star athlete. If he achieves that success by sabotaging another player behind the scenes or cheating, then virtue is not present. He has surrendered to vice, acting out of pride and envy rather than fortitude and justice.

Recognize and Accept

Accept the fact that you are human, and as a human you have fears—fears about your spirituality and even fears you don't know you have. Are you afraid to let people know that you are a practicing Catholic? Are you worried about what they will think of you? If so, admit it, confess it to God, and pray for the strength to love Him more than you love worldly acceptance. Are you afraid of being wrong? Even in matters of faith? This may be a good thing if it causes you to study and learn, but don't allow your newfound knowledge to undermine your humility. The Pharisees knew a lot too. Are you afraid of losing something? Your comfortable lifestyle? Your group of cool friends? Your position of authority? Are you afraid to tell your son, father, or brother, "I love you"? None of this is unnatural, and you are not alone in feeling this way. But recognize your fear and admit its effect on your life, its influence on your actions. If you do not recognize and accept that your fears exist, how can you ever fight them?

Prepare

Fortitude is virtuous when it is applied to the objective truth as taught by Jesus Christ and His church. First Peter 3:15 states, "Always be ready to give an explanation to anyone who asks you for a reason for your hope." This means to **think about why God is important to you**. Why is your faith important? Why is God important to society and the world? What is your worldview? Is there real truth that never changes? Is law, order, and structure built into everything in existence? Is God real? Did Jesus die for your sins? Did His resurrection bring about the possibility of eternal life for you and me? **What do you believe?** If you need to find a basic outline of Catholic belief, I suggest starting with the Nicene Creed. Whether you know it or not, we recite the basics of our faith every Sunday at Mass.

Anchored on this shared foundation, we should also think through the social issues occurring today. What is the purpose of wealth? Is abortion merely a choice, or is it something more? Is marriage by definition between one man and one woman? If not, who gets to define the boundaries of what marriage is? Who creates laws and why? What are they founded on? What is the ultimate law or authority?

Fortitude must be directed. We prepare to practice fortitude by praying for God's wisdom and guidance to know what to stand up for. Without the truth to guide us, we will be pulled along with the current of society. And who needs fortitude then?

Practice Discipline

Holy Mother Church in her wisdom sets aside two penitential times each year, Advent and Lent. These seasons invite us to prepare our hearts and minds to fully absorb the gravity and transformative power of the signature moments of salvation: the coming of Christ, and His death and resurrection. Our faith recognizes that we need to be reminded to discipline ourselves and sacrifice—which means more than just contributing to the collection basket. Discipline leads to transformation.

I am a long-distance runner, and so I often think about my spiritual journey in these terms. For example, what am I willing to sacrifice in order to qualify for the Boston Marathon? Usually this discipline covers about three to four months of training. The sacrifice and the training prepare me for the actual race when it comes. If I have prepared and sacrificed well, usually the race goes as desired. But if I cut corners, I will not be ready for the race. Learn to give up things that may be pleasant or desirous now, knowing that you are building strength and discipline for when the real race comes. In a marathon, the real challenge starts around the 23rd mile when I am severely tired and uncomfortable. The previous hard training and sacrifice helps me to endure what is to come in the final 3.2 miles. The training does not make the feat easier, but it becomes possible. My muscles and mind have been fortified enough to do what is necessary.

Ensure Compassion Is Present

To be clear, the virtue of fortitude is not a single-minded human effort to press on and move forward through any obstacle regardless of the consequences. Strength, courage, and fortitude are always interwoven with compassion, mercy, and love for other people. To truly move outward and away from our self-protective and self-promoting tendencies, we require great courage, great fortitude, and great love. Think of those who travel into the toughest parts of the city to feed and care for the homeless. Think of the army medic on the battlefield fighting to save lives and bind up wounds rather than inflict them. Think of the expectant parents who learn that their unborn child will be disabled mentally or physically yet move forward with the pregnancy, ready to love their child and create a family. Think of the elderly man sitting at the bedside of his sick wife, holding her hand and being present. This is fortitude wrapped in loving care. May we all practice it fully!

Catholic Bushido

One of my favorite books is *The Silmarillion* by J.R.R. Tolkien. In this book Tolkien gives an account of creation that includes beings that resemble the angels and fallen angels of our Catholic faith. One of the good angels who comes to take part in the battles between good and evil is Tulkas. He is strong and swift, great and valiant in battle, and whether he is competing in sport or in war, Tulkas laughs.[6]

May we as men recognize the fear that stands in our path, great or small. May we learn not to run from it but to turn and, with God's grace, laugh. "For God did not give us a spirit of cowardice, but rather of power, love and self-control" (2 Timothy 1:7).

Remember that fortitude is the strength to do what is right and good. Keep the words from the Catechism close to your heart; may fortitude strengthen you and let you stand firm as you resist, overcome, and conquer every foe you face. And may we do so with love, compassion, and mercy.

Prayer

Loving and eternal God, make me a man after Your own heart. A man who is honest with himself and who desires to be strong enough to become who You want him to be. Help us, Lord God, to practice fortitude in the times of trial and struggle; help us to continue on when the way is not clear. Give us the endurance we need so that we can fully become who You have created us to be and inspire others to do the same. In Jesus' holy name we pray. Amen.

Scripture for Reflection

"Peter said to him in reply, 'Lord, if it is you, command me to come to you on the water.' He said, 'Come.' Peter got out of the boat and began to walk on the water toward Jesus. But when he saw how [strong] the wind was he became frightened; and, beginning to sink, he cried out, 'Lord, save me!' Immediately Jesus stretched out his hand and caught him, and said to him, 'O you of little faith, why did you doubt?'"

—*Matthew 14:28–31*

"Therefore, my beloved brothers, be firm, steadfast, always fully devoted to the work of the Lord, knowing that in the Lord your labor is not in vain."

—*1 Corinthians 15:58*

"Be on your guard, stand firm in the faith, be courageous, be strong."

—*1 Corinthians 16:13*

"Do not fear, you shall not be put to shame; do not be discouraged, you shall not be disgraced. For the shame of your youth you shall forget, the reproach of your widowhood no longer remember."

—*Isaiah 54:4*

"Though harshly treated, he submitted
and did not open his mouth;
Like a lamb led to slaughter
or a sheep silent before shearers,
he did not open his mouth."

—*Isaiah 53:7*

"I command you: be strong and steadfast! Do not fear nor be dismayed, for the LORD, your God, is with you wherever you go."

—*Joshua 1:9*

Wisdom of the Saints

"Fear is such a powerful emotion for humans that when we allow it to take us over, it drives compassion right out of our hearts."

—*St. Thomas Aquinas*[7]

"Laugh and grow strong."

—*St. Ignatius of Loyola*[8]

"A sacrifice to be real must cost, must hurt, and must empty ourselves. Give yourself fully to God. He will use you to accomplish great things on the condition that you believe much more in his love than in your weakness."

—*St. Teresa of Calcutta*[9]

Questions for Reflection

1. Why is fortitude necessary? How does it help me live the spiritual life?
2. What things am I afraid of? How can I apply this virtue to overcome my fears?
3. Does the practice of fortitude require me to be tough and hardcore? Why or why not?
4. What are some ways in which fortitude is related to compassion?
5. What can I do to develop greater fortitude in my own life?

7

Faith

The Question and the Light

I can clearly remember one night when I was about 18 years old and cooling off after an argument with my girlfriend. The specifics aren't important, but I was having one of those moments as a teenager where I felt disenfranchised with everything and everyone. I felt alone and, for lack of a better word, empty. I was not necessarily despairing, but I was certainly not in a positive frame of mind.

That night I drove alone through the parking lot of our local high school. I can see the lights and feel the speedbumps as if I'm there now. Then it happened. In an instant, the question rang so clearly in my mind: "What is this all about? Why am I even here?" I heard the question like a bell going off in my head or heart. Philosophers might call this moment my existential awakening: I was suddenly clearly aware that my life was happening *now*, and I wanted to know why.

In his encyclical *Fides et ratio* (Faith and Reason), St. Pope John Paul II says, "The truth comes initially to the human being as a question: Does life have a meaning? Where is it going?"[1] The saint tells us that faith begins with the open and humble search for truth—truth about our own existence. And when this question arises in the human heart, it demands an answer. We can, and often do, choose to bury this question under alcohol, sex, drugs, human success, or other diversions. But the question remains. It constantly burns into us, and the only relieving salve is the humble and honest search for the truth. My wife Angela has always said, "Encourage people to seek the truth." If they do, they will uncover the right questions and the right answers in God's time for them.

Truth

Truth does exist, even if you cannot see it. It exists outside of, and is not dependent upon, you or your understanding. For example, let's say you have two four-foot sections of 2x4 lumber. You stand one up on end, take the other, and lay it on top of the first so that it forms a T shape. If you've balanced the sections properly, the boards will remain standing when you take your hand away. However, if you try to shift the top horizontal 2x4 along the vertical section so that the boards form an upside-down L, the horizontal piece will never stay up because it is not supported correctly. Regardless of what you believe about gravity or physics, this will be the result. The laws undergirding our physical world existed before any of us. This truth exists outside of, and without reliance on, our knowledge or experience. I see this as similar to faith in God. When Moses saw the burning bush and asked God what he should say when the Israelites asked him for God's name, God said to tell them "I Am" has sent you. "I Am" is existence itself. God *is* existence. Like truth, His existence is not contingent upon our understanding or belief. It just is.

Abraham's Example

> "Then God said: 'Take your son Isaac, your only one, whom you love, and go to the land of Moriah. There offer him up as a burnt offering on one of the heights that I will point out to you...' When they came to the place of which God had told him, Abraham built an altar there and arranged the wood on it. Next, he bound his son Isaac, and put him on top of the wood on the altar" (Genesis 22:2, 9).

In the time between these two verses of Scripture, Isaac asks his father Abraham why they brought wood and kindling for a sacrifice but no sheep. Isaac does not know he is to be the sacrifice. Abraham tells his son that God will provide the sheep for the burnt offering. Was Abraham lying to his son to hide the fact that God had ordered him to sacrifice Isaac? Was he trying to keep Isaac from attempting an escape, or did he really have that much blind trust in God? Did he truly believe, without proof, that God would provide a way out—for both of them?

Abraham carries the title of "our father in faith." Throughout his life and through his actions, he demonstrated a deep and fully committed faith. Genesis 22:10 says that after Abraham put Isaac on top of the wood, he reached and pulled out his dagger in order to slaughter his son. It was not until that moment that the angel of God stopped him. God's demand of Abraham required him to go all the way in his intention, but not quite all the way in his action. Abraham went right to the brink, then God provided the way out. Was Abraham able to trust God in this way through mere determination? Did he tie up his son and lay him on the woodpile out of human strength? Was it a characteristic Abraham had, a trait passed on from his parents? Could I do it? Could you?

What Is the Theological Virtue of Faith?

The theological virtues are sometimes known as the infused virtues, meaning that it is God's grace alone that makes them possible. This sanctifying grace is given to us at our baptism.[2] Faith, then, is the theological virtue by which we believe God and all that He has said and revealed to us through Scripture and the instruction of the Catholic Church.[3] True faith, in this sense, is unobtainable by man alone; it is only by the gift of God's grace at work in us that the seed is planted and the space created where this faith can sprout. Abraham therefore was empowered by God to believe and to trust.

The Catechism says that the theological virtues are infused into us to make us *capable* of acting as God's children. In other words, the seed is planted, but we somehow must act upon it; we must choose in our souls to accept this spark, flicker, or sprout of faith and not ignore it but nurture it, protect it, and coax it into growth. By virtue of our free will, we as human beings are given the gift and responsibility of choice. Abraham could have chosen not to believe God and ignored the demand to sacrifice his son. He could have stayed home and not started on the journey. But no, Abraham chose the unknown path, a path on which he was not in control. He was infused with faith and chose to nurture that gift. As we acquiesce to this faith that enters our hearts, it leads us to freely give our lives over in service to God. We are wholly and totally in need of God for our faith—we cannot nurture our faith until God gives us the seed. But He is lavish in His gift giving. Praise His name!

How Do We Know?

In *Fides et ratio*, St. John Paul II says that faith and reason are two different ways of "knowing." Your individual experience of faith forms your way of knowing spiritual truth. These sacred experiences are very personal and often hard to effectively communicate to another person. The words we use are only heard, while an experience often engages all of the senses, including our spirit. We can easily discuss scientific facts like the temperatures at which water freezes or turns to steam because we share a familiarity with all the associated concepts. But we may struggle to find a shared, understood language for talking about matters of faith.

Faith and spiritual events are a part of my very existence. And so, despite the difficulty, I want to try to explain an episode of my existence to you in such a way that you will vicariously know and feel what I experienced. In 1994, the Billy Graham Crusade came to Cleveland Municipal Stadium. My wife Angela and I took part in training classes prior to the Crusade in order to be witnesses and evangelists during the altar call. I didn't complete the training process, so while my wife had a defined role to play, I just attended the Crusade with her. I will never forget being there, sitting in this huge stadium filled with people. When Billy Graham invited people to come down onto the field and give their lives to Christ, I experienced this powerful draw and internal pulling to go down. It was almost physical. This drawing of people to come forward seemed to move throughout the stadium, pulling at the attendees, drawing them down. For me this was a very personal and palpable experience, yet one that I experienced with thousands of other people. Now, while we all experienced this same event, I am sure that if asked, we would all try to explain it a little differently. Sometimes the limitations of our human language inhibit our ability to put these faith experiences into words. We just can't make another person experience what we did at that moment in time. That moment was real, and we all experienced it, but the *way* we "know it" is ours alone. This is how faith works.

.. .ɔ mysterious. It is cold, hard truth, yet at the same time not my personal possession to control. Its revealing truths are shared by millions as we walk together, yet completely personal in how it applies to each individual life.

We Are Called

But when and where is faith found? How does it start? Is there anything that I can do to develop faith?

In Thomas Merton's book *Thoughts in Solitude*, he says, "There will never be any awakening in me unless I am called out of darkness by Him Who is my light. Only He Who is life is able to raise the dead. And unless He names me, I remain dead…. My life is a listening, His is a speaking. My salvation is to hear and respond."[4] This call of God raises the dead, brings life, and saves us who need saving.

But are you and I prepared to hear? Many in today's world rely on their own voice, or voices that sound similar to their own and speak as they do. I believe that Satan knows this. He also knows that darkness cannot overcome the light, that deceit cannot be maintained forever. At some point a lie eats itself and is revealed. The devil cannot extinguish truth. So his plan is to hide the truth in a forest of counterfeits that flash and call our names. They appeal to us by telling us the things that we in our fallen nature want to be true: *Happiness and fulfillment are found in careers and money. Your happiness is based on you alone.* The sheer number of messages the world asks us to look at and listen to will eventually beat us into submission; we give up and say, oh, there are so many, they are all so similar—one must be as good as another. Our challenge is to emerge from the forest of comfortable half-truths, humbly listening for the voice of Christ calling us out of darkness.

When Jesus traveled to Bethany and stood in front of the closed tomb of Lazarus, He called for His friend. He called him by name and told him to come forth out of the tomb and back to the living. Lazarus responded to Christ's call; he came out of the tomb and lived for many years afterward (according to tradition). But think about this event: Jesus did not open the tomb, walk in with His apostles, and carry Lazarus out. Christ stood outside and called him, and Lazarus heard His call. Lazarus heard the voice of God speaking to him alone, and he responded. No one else can hear God's call for you. You have to hear it on your own. The call echoes in the depth of your tomb; your name is spoken to you personally. You must make the choice to respond and walk out of the tomb and into new life.

The call of Christ brings our faith to life. But how do we hear it? Romans 10:14 says, "But how can they call on Him in whom they have not believed? And how can they believe in Him of whom they have not heard? And how can they hear without someone to preach?" Then verse 17 gives the answer: "Thus faith comes from what is heard." We have to hear about Christ to have faith in Him.

At baptism, the priest instructs the child's parents and godparents to bring him up and teach him the ways of faith. To conclude the rite, the priest hands a candle that was lit from the Easter candle to the parents, saying, "Parents and godparents, this light is entrusted to you to be kept burning brightly." He is referring to the light of faith in Christ. In the company of our family of believers (in our home and in our church), we first hear about spiritual truths. This is where the call of faith begins for many of us. It is a great responsibility.

What Do We Believe?

What are the things that, as Catholics, we believe by faith? The following is the Nicene Creed that we recite at every Mass:

I believe in one God,

the Father almighty,

maker of heaven and earth,

of all things visible and invisible.

I believe in one Lord Jesus Christ,

the Only Begotten Son of God,

born of the Father before all ages.

God from God, Light from Light,

true God from true God,

begotten, not made, consubstantial with the Father;

through him all things were made.

For us men and for our salvation

he came down from heaven,

and by the Holy Spirit was incarnate of the Virgin Mary,

and became man.

For our sake he was crucified under Pontius Pilate,

he suffered death and was buried,

and rose again on the third day

in accordance with the Scriptures.

He ascended into heaven

and is seated at the right hand of the Father.

He will come again in glory

to judge the living and the dead

and his kingdom will have no end.

I believe in the Holy Spirit, the Lord, the giver of life,

who proceeds from the Father and the Son,

who with the Father and the Son is adored and glorified,

who has spoken through the prophets.

I believe in one, holy, catholic and apostolic Church.

I confess one Baptism for the forgiveness of sins

and I look forward to the resurrection of the dead

and the life of the world to come. Amen.[5]

We believe that the Eucharist is the real body and blood of Jesus Christ—that bread and wine become Jesus. How do we explain this? We can quote the Bread of Life Discourse found in John 6, but the truth of this sacrament requires faith and the acceptance of mystery, as do most of the things in the Nicene Creed. Yet many of us have had very personal experiences of God, of the Holy Spirit moving us or guiding us in some way. When these spiritual encounters happen, they help us to accept the many truths of faith, even those that we have not yet experienced.

Examples of Faith

Mother Teresa

St. Teresa of Calcutta is one of my heroes. I may be an endurance athlete, ex-football player, and blackbelt, but this frail, shriveled old woman is so inspiring to me. She truly is. And it is God's work in me that has made it this way. Let me assure you, the "human accomplishments" I listed do not require nearly as much strength as living a faithful life. God has placed in my heart a recognition of how weak I really am and how strong faith is. There are many examples from her life that I could point to, but one that speaks volumes is the knowledge that she struggled internally, in her spirit, during the last 35 years of her life. She felt abandoned. In one letter to her priest confessor, she wrote, "Now Father, since 49 or 50 this terrible sense of loss, this untold darkness, this loneliness, this continual longing for God which gives me that pain deep down in my heart. Darkness is such that I really do not see, neither with my mind nor with my reason. The place of God in my soul is blank."[6] How could she continue on like this for so long? Her faith in God's direction and in His call had so transformed and molded her over the years that even though she felt dry, dark, and distant from God, she continued to wholly give herself to the work she was called to. The experiences of a life of faith—and the hidden, unknown presence of God in them—transform us and can make us into real agents of change in this world. Some will even become saints.

Beth Nimmo

On April 20, 1999, two students arrived at Columbine High School with guns, pipe bombs, and a plan that would devastate families and communities and shock the world. One young lady, Rachel Joy Scott, was killed that day along with a dozen others. Her mother, Beth Nimmo, received a letter from the mother of one of the shooters. Beth responded by reaching out to this woman and meeting with her. After all, thought Beth, this woman also lost a child, her son.[7] Her faith in God and belief in His message gave her a compassion that went outside of herself. She found compassion for the mother of the boy that shot and killed her daughter. Would she be able to explain this movement of God's grace in her heart using human language? Could she explain it to us in such a way as we could all feel it and know it ourselves? Probably not, but her faith was nonetheless true, and the proof of it was in her actions.

St. Thomas More

St. Thomas was Lord Chancellor in the court of King Henry VIII in England. He was a trusted and devout man who knew that the sacrament of marriage is an unbreakable bond. He believed the word of God and the teaching of the Catholic Church—he had faith. King Henry wanted Thomas's help in persuading the pope to annul his marriage. Not only did St. Thomas refuse to sign the letter to the pope, but he also refused to attend the coronation of King Henry VIII's new wife. Sometime later, Thomas refused to acknowledge Henry as head of the church. The bitter king locked Thomas in the tower of London and finally ordered his execution.

Stories of these saints can seem so far removed from our own lives, almost as if they are fictitious stories. But they're not. St. Thomas More was punished by his government, by the king himself, because he chose to take actions based on truth and faith. We too can be placed in positions where we're told to ignore the real truth and exchange it for a counterfeit created by man. This can happen when an employer asks you to cheat a customer, when a friend asks you to lie to his wife for him, when your child breaks the law. Truth and goodness do not change; they exist outside of us. St. Thomas believed and acted accordingly.

Renewalists

At my home parish, we have been holding men's renewal retreats for the last several years. The retreats last one and a half days with the men staying overnight. We call the men who attend "renewalists." Each group of renewalists is unique, made up of men from different backgrounds, education levels, likes, and dislikes. On the opening morning, men share a little about themselves, including the reason why they came. Across the years, more than one man has said his reason for attending is because his wife asked him to. Others will say, "I don't know," while others will have very specific reasons, perhaps due to something that recently happened in their lives or in the life of a loved one. Sometimes men come because they have just become fathers or have just awoken to the importance of their role as fathers.

But in every case, God's grace is the true compelling force at work. Whether these men can explain it or not, something deep inside persuaded them to sign up, get up early on a Saturday morning, and come. As a member of the organizing team, I then receive the privilege of walking with these men through the weekend. Some of these mentoring friendships may continue for weeks, months, or years afterward. These retreat weekends are filled with opportunities for the attendees' faith to change, expand, grow, or come into being. And as I watch, my own faith is renewed. At the end of the weekend, the renewalists have an opportunity to share some of what they experienced. The majority of these men are thoroughly amazed at the new vision and perspective they have on life. They have new expectations for what God will do in their lives and within their family members. There is a joyful strengthening that occurs. An optimism about what lies ahead combined with a confidence that recognizes the simplicity of faith and God's desire for us. As these men's faith is strengthened, so is my faith and the faith of the other team members. This is one of the mysteries of faith: it is highly personal and yet fully communal.

What Can I Do?

There is nothing you can do to initiate faith yourself. Faith is a gift of God's grace. You cannot force this infusion of faith. However, you can respond to God's call and further prepare your spirit to receive and grow stronger in faith.

Prayer

As always, the first thing to do to grow in virtue is foster a solid personal prayer life. This prayer life forms the basis of our relationship with God. All relationships require both speaking and listening. It is no different with God. I find that, for me, the listening part is the most irregular. For me to listen, my mind must be free from other cares or concerns, which is pretty rare. But this ability can be improved with consistent practice. That is a challenge I have to tackle each day.

If you are new to the speaking part, there is a formula that you may find helpful. I do not know where it originated, but it follows the acronym ACTS (like the book of Acts), which stands for **A**doration, **C**ontrition, **T**hanksgiving, and **S**upplication. During a prayer time, go through each of these different types of prayer. Start with adoring God for who He is, then confess to Him what you are sorry for. Move on to thanking Him for what He has done for you this day, and then ask Him for the things you need for yourself, the world, and those around you. It could sound something like this:

> "Oh God, my Creator, You are the giver of all things, and all good things come from You. I praise You for who You are. Forgive me, Lord, for being selfish and angry today with my family; change my heart and give me the grace to do better. Thank You for the warm house that we have to live in and the food that we have to eat every day. Thank You for my job and all of its challenges; it helps me to provide for and care for my family. I ask that You would bring peace to our world, that You would

bring healing to my father if it is Your will, and that You would help me, my wife, and my sons to hear Your voice and grow closer to You. Amen."

Participation

Just like with any other area of desired growth, being around like-minded people striving for the same goal helps. Going to Mass every week is essential. First of all, God deserves our worship, and so it is our duty. But it is also to our benefit. God brings His people together, giving us the chance to see each other's struggles so that we can all help each other along the way in faithfulness. Participate in the celebration of the other sacraments as well, including reconciliation. Join a ministry such as serving the poor. Just take a small action, one small step, and you'll be pleasantly surprised how things open up to you.

Study

Read Scripture daily. Know what it is you believe. Know it so well that you can communicate it to others. The website for the United States Conference of Catholic Bishops (USCCB.org) posts the daily Mass readings, with the entire Bible also available for daily use. Ignorance of Scripture is ignorance of Christ, as St. Jerome said. When we read the word of God, we hear His voice speaking to us. We can read a book or section of the Bible multiple times and get a different inspiration for our lives each time we do it. This can actually be a part of our listening prayer. A technique called *Lectio Divina* instructs us to read a small section of God's word and then meditate on it, allowing the words God has written to open up in our hearts.

We can also do more formal Scripture studies; many times the best way to start with this is to join a Scripture study group. In these groups we get to hear how God's word speaks to all of us. I have also been in groups where we have studied the lives of certain saints, learned about icons (religious paintings), or studied the Catechism. All of these things point us toward God, helping us to know Him better to more clearly hear His voice in our hearts.

Take Time to Listen

God wants to communicate with us. But we need to be ready and prepared to hear. In my experience, the hearing is more of an internal movement of my heart and soul rather than something auditory like a voice from the sky. As I prepare to listen, I must put away thoughts about myself and my own desires. In preparing to listen, I must willfully choose to hear what God wants to say and nothing more. I find it very hard, almost impossible, to hear God's call or be aware of His direction when my mind and spirit are agitated. Although it is rare to be perfectly at peace, we can still try. I think the best way to hear from God is to specifically set aside a time for listening to God. A very good friend of mine works across the street from a Catholic church. He goes there regularly for daily Mass, but he will also go there and just sit in front of the Blessed Sacrament. He sits there with God, and he listens. I think this is a great idea that I am trying to incorporate into my own life. If this is not possible for you, then find your own time and place. Make it simple and uncomplicated, whether sitting somewhere or taking a walk by yourself. Let's just take time to listen. Our loving God will speak, and our faith will be strengthened.

Share It with Others

We do not need to stand on a box in the public square and shout for all to hear, but we do have to share our faith with others. We can do this by word and deed. Our faith will grow stronger when we share it and see others grow in their faith as a result. As parents, it is our responsibility to share our faith with our children, but we can also share it with other family members, friends, and even co-workers.

In the end, faith is an intensely personal journey that we can't make alone. But we all have to make a decision at some point, a personal choice, to take the first step. In his series "Catholicism," Bishop Robert Barron makes a very interesting statement. He says that the person of Jesus requires from each of us a conscious choice. As Jesus portrays Himself as the Son of God, Bishop Barron says He leaves us no middle ground. Either Jesus Christ is who He says He is—the Son of God—or he is a deranged, dangerous, and mentally unstable person.[8] Through my faith and life experiences; through prayer and my reading of Scripture; through my relationships with my wife, family, and friends; through the horrible things that have happened in my life; through the blessings that I have experienced; through my awareness of all that is good and all that is evil in the world; through my failings, my faults, and my successes; through the sum total of this current existence God has given me, I can tell you that I believe Jesus Christ is the Son of God and my savior. What is your choice?

Catholic Bushido

Be prepared to step out into the unknown. You may be asked to go someplace or do something you have never done before, great or small. It will likely be revealed to you in the mundane and cumulative activities of your daily living. This is where you must be prepared to listen and hear. No one else can tell you what God's purpose and will for you is. You can be told that it exists and that it is real, but you must listen, hear it for yourself, and respond. The joy and comfort God gives to you in this is that though you listen alone, you are surrounded by a community of faith engaged in the same effort. Offer support to your brothers and sisters and receive their comfort in return.

Scripture for Reflection

"For by grace you have been saved through faith, and this is not from you; it is the gift of God, it is not from works, so no one may boast."

—*Ephesians 2:8–9*

"Although you have not seen him you love him; even though you do not see him now yet believe in him, you rejoice with an indescribable and glorious joy, as you attain the goal of [your] faith, the salvation of your souls."

—*1 Peter 1:8–9*

"Faith is the realization of what is hoped for and evidence of things not seen."

—Hebrews 11:1

"For God so loved the world that he gave his only Son, so that everyone who believes in him might not perish but might have eternal life."

—John 3:16

"Jesus said to him, 'Have you come to believe because you have seen me? Blessed are those who have not seen and have believed.'"

—John 20:29

"For this reason I kneel before the Father, from whom every family in heaven and on earth is named, that he may grant you in accord with the riches of his glory to be strengthened with power through his Spirit in the inner self, and that Christ may dwell in your hearts through faith; that you, rooted and grounded in love, may have strength to comprehend with all the holy ones what is the breadth and length and height and depth, and to know the love of Christ that surpasses knowledge, so that you may be filled with all the fullness of God."

—Ephesians 3:14–19

Wisdom of the Saints

"To one who has faith, no explanation is necessary. To one without faith, no explanation is possible."

—*St. Thomas Aquinas*[9]

"The most beautiful act of faith is the one made in darkness, in sacrifice, and with extreme effort."

—*St. Padre Pio*[10]

"Error indeed is never set forth in its naked deformity, lest, being thus exposed, it should at once be detected. But it is craftily decked out in an attractive dress, so as, by its outward form, to make it appear to the inexperienced more true than truth itself."

—*St. Irenaeus of Lyon*[11]

Questions for Reflection

1. How would you explain Saint John Paul II's teaching that faith is another way of knowing?
2. Can we obtain faith on our own?
3. How is faith both personal and communal at the same time?
4. How can I support and foster faith in myself and others?
5. How does faith impact the ways that I act and interact with others? Give examples.

8

Hope

Always New

have the sense—not the thought, because it doesn't come as words—that something better exists. Something good, a relieving balm, a warm rest, a gentle word or touch. The sense that this is not the only and final reality. Where I sit today, the pain that I feel, the unanchored drifting of my life—this is not my destiny. Meaning exists. I don't know everything, I cannot see where it all ends or why it all started—but I hope.

As an infant, in the late 1960s, I was baptized and confirmed as a Byzantine Catholic at St. Eugene's in Bedford, Ohio. About five years later, the summer before I entered first grade, we moved to the country. The rural area we moved to was without a Byzantine Catholic Church, so we attended the local Roman Catholic parish. (This is the same parish I have been attending now for 45 years. It is the parish where my wife went through the Rite of Christian Initiation of Adults and became Catholic and both of my sons were raised receiving the sacraments.) As a cradle Catholic child (both Byzantine and Roman), I went to Mass (or the Divine Liturgy) with my family somewhat regularly and always at Christmas and Easter. But it didn't go much further than that. There were no discussions about faith and moral issues around the dinner table, and we didn't have family prayer time together. There was no underlying deep faith structure serving as a compass to guide us through our crises and dilemmas.

My father, God rest his soul, was an alcoholic; he worked, and most nights after work he drank. Sometimes just one drink, oftentimes more. But he was a professional with a college degree and a good job. Throughout my childhood, I was never in material need; we always had a warm home, food, clothes, and working vehicles. None of my basic physical needs were neglected. He provided a good life for our family. What we were missing, though, was stability.

The thing about living with an alcoholic is that there's really no security at home. You never know what emotion is going to be governing their behavior when they walk through the door. And you're never certain when they will arrive, so inside you're always a little on edge, waiting, and at the same time not knowing what you're waiting for.

Whenever I talk about this part of my life, about my relationship with my father, I feel the need to balance it by saying that my father did some great things for me too. Things that really helped me in my life. But his drinking, and his behavior when he drank, ruled our relationship and our family. As a seven or eight-year-old boy, how could I understand the process of working through these thoughts and feelings? I was confused. As I grew into a teenager, I didn't have to go through confirmation preparation like some of my friends because in the Byzantine Catholic Church I had been baptized and confirmed at the same time. I was no longer required by my parents to attend Sunday school or to go to Mass every weekend, and so I didn't.

From my early teens to my early twenties, I didn't really think about my faith. Church, religion, and God were not priorities for me. I was rarely at home and rarely attended church on Sunday mornings. I was not interested in hearing about what Christ would want for and from me. It wasn't that I was consciously rejecting God. I was just not thinking about Him at all. I was focused one hundred percent on what I wanted for myself. In my mind, everything revolved around me. Interestingly enough, though, there were still times that popped up out of nowhere in which I chose not to do certain things because of an internal voice guiding me toward the wise choice. Sometimes I even remembered to pray. These occasions were like lightning strikes of conscience. Looking back, I interpret this as an example of receiving God's grace through the sacraments during my childhood. Even though I didn't think about it in these terms, at strategic times His grace would jump to the forefront of my conscience and burst forth, forcing me into some action, or in some cases restraint.

There Is Something More

I frequently think about my relationship with my father, both its good and bad elements. Yes, there were times when he came home drunk and was unpleasant to my mother, brothers, sisters, and me. But I also experienced wonderful times with my father, some profound and unexpected, others simple in nature but no less significant. For example, during the summer months we would cook out every Sunday for our family dinners, and my dad would always give me the first bite of steak off of the grill. I knew that he loved me and my family, but he had human and spiritual struggles of his own.

Because I grew up experiencing these contradictory ways of living and relating with my father, I developed a hunger and deep appreciation for the good times. In a purely human and somewhat broken way, I think I learned to experience hope. I hoped my dad would come home in a good mood. I hoped for what could be, for what I knew existed and was good. I can't say that I consciously thought of it in these terms, but hope was there in my subconscious wanting something more, something better. Since I had little to no guidance as a teenager, my desire for a better life led me to search for it through selfish behaviors. I tried to fill this desire for happiness with the things the world offered. Over time, and through a number of painful experiences, I found that the world could not fill this need. But when I was finally able to hear God calling my name, this hope for something better was transformed and elevated into a greater and truer hope in the new life Christ brings.

This transition from human struggle to joy in Christ is described in the following words from St. Paul's Letter to the Romans:

> "Not only that, but we even boast of our afflictions, knowing that affliction produces endurance, and endurance, proven character, and proven character, hope, **and hope does not disappoint**, because the love of God has been poured out into our hearts through the holy spirit that has been given to us" (Romans 5:3–5).

Yes, we emerge from struggle with the abundance of God being *poured* out into us like a flood.

Hope Transformed and Elevated

In paragraph 1817 of the *Catechism of the Catholic Church*, hope is defined as "the theological virtue by which we desire the kingdom of heaven and eternal life as our happiness, placing our trust in Christ's promises and relying not on our own strength, but on the help of the grace of the Holy Spirit."[1] The Catechism goes on to say that our desire for or aspiration to happiness has been placed into us by God. We want to be happy, and we desire for things to be good; this is our created nature. The virtue of hope, however, takes this natural, worldly hope in earthly things and purifies it and orders it toward eternal life. So, like the other theological virtues, this one too is placed in us by God's grace alone. It cannot be obtained by practice and learning. This elevated hope allows us to see that eternal life and relationship with God is the ultimate thing we can hope for and desire. All other good things on this earth are only a small foreshadowing or taste of the ultimate good of life with our Creator. When infused into us, the theological virtue of hope buoys us up like a bobber dragging us up from the depths to the surface where we can breathe again. It pulls us onward, giving us energy and endurance, courage, and strength. The virtue of hope fuels us to carry on in this world, bringing the message of the gospel to all who will hear it, while at the same time waiting on eternal life and the wedding feast to which we ourselves are called. Ephesians 1:18 says, "May the eyes of your heart be enlightened, that you may know what is the hope that belongs to his call."

Hope in Today's World

Oh, that we could all be a little more hopeful, that we could all look outward a little further and recognize how much goodness exists. That the selfish scales through which I see the world would fall from my eyes. If I could only have the grace to experience the warmth of the summer sun on my face and allow it to create a smile of gratitude for that instant without the need to own it.

My father-in-law Gil is an inspiration. He has become a father figure to me, and I love him dearly. Gil is not particularly religious, but he consciously tries to live each day of his life with optimism. "Keep on the Sunny Side of Life" is one of his favorite songs. The first verse goes like this:

There's a dark and a troubled side of life,

But there's a bright and sunny side too.

Though you meet with the darkness and strife,

the sunny side you also may view.²

Doesn't this song sound as if hope is woven through it like a hidden thread? And don't we all have those people in our lives, like Gil, that we wish we could imitate at times? I have come to believe, through my own experiences, that much of this human attitude of gratitude and hopefulness is chosen. I also believe that we can choose the opposite attitude. Just to be clear, while the choice of being hopeful is available to everyone in every situation, it may not be an easy choice to make. Some people will face more harrowing circumstances than others. Someone who loses a child, for example, will find choosing gratitude and hope to be far more difficult than someone who recently lost a fruit tree growing in their back yard—and I think we recognize this. **However, we highly admire those people that go through difficult tragedy and come out the other end hopeful and helpful**. Or those who, even in the midst of suffering themselves, offer hope. In his book *Man's Search for Meaning*, Viktor Frankl, an Austrian psychiatrist who survived the Holocaust, gave this insight:

"We who lived in the concentration camps can remember the men who walked through the huts comforting others, giving away their last piece of bread. They may have been few in number, but they offer sufficient proof that everything can be taken from a man but one thing: the last of the human freedoms...to choose one's attitude in any given set of circumstances, to choose one's own way."[3]

Those who choose to be hopeful and strong, in effect, help me to choose the same. Hope breeds hope; it's contagious. In many of the stories from Scripture, both Old and New Testament, the desert was the place of transformation. Some were led into the desert, and some went on their own accord, but in all cases it seems that it is in the desert that we, as human beings, can be transformed.

In the book of 1 Kings, Elijah the prophet flees for his life from Jezebel. He flees into the wilderness. There, emotionally crushed, he sits down under a broom tree and prays for death. But instead of death, an angel comes and gives him food and water. Elijah needs strength for the journey that God has appointed for him. After Elijah eats and drinks his fill, he walks for forty days and forty nights to Mount Horeb. It is here that God shows Himself to Elijah in one of my favorite sections of Scripture. In 1 Kings 19:11–13, Elijah is commanded to stand on the mountain before the Lord. Elijah sees rock-crushing winds, earthquakes, and fires, but as the Scripture says, the Lord is not in them. But "after the fire, a light silent sound." When Elijah hears this, he hides his face. Elijah goes from despair in the wilderness to hope and purpose, at which time God reveals to him a truth about who He really is.

Examples of Hope

The Exodus

The Hebrew people at the time of the Exodus left Egypt and followed Moses into the desert. They left behind slavery, certainly, but also security. They left behind what they knew. They left, because they hoped in the promise God had given them through Moses. Hope of freedom from bondage, hope for the promised land that God would lead them to.

I'm a Survivor

When she was 23 years old, my wife was diagnosed with a rare bladder disease called Interstitial Cystitis (IC). This disease results in open sores on the inner lining of the bladder. The pain flares are so severe and can linger, unrelenting, for such a long time that many IC victims commit suicide. I watched Angela walk on her tip-toes because the mere impact of her foot against the floor would jar her bladder and cause pain. When driving anywhere, we had to find smooth roads to limit the jostling. I also watched as she underwent numerous and painful "installations" of chemicals into her bladder that were intended to burn away parts of the inner lining in an effort to promote healing. What kept her going? In my opinion she is certainly an example of fortitude in action, but I also look at how she embraced the faith that we share—I know she had hope. It was in there, not as some bubbly, carefree anticipation of the future, but as a lifeline, one she would not let go of. I watched as she endured all of this while refusing to stop living her life. The life God had given her. Our hope in God's mysterious plan brings great endurance, and Angela provided a perfect example of this.

I Had an Accident

Joni Eareckson Tada was in a diving accident in 1967 that left her bound to a wheelchair as a quadriplegic. Joni spent years in rehabilitation, and during that time she learned to paint with a brush between her teeth. Joni has spent a lifetime encouraging people and bringing them hope because of what she was able to overcome. She is the founder and CEO of Joni and Friends International Disability Center and is an author and sought-after speaker. Her accomplishments are too many to list here, but she is one of those people we can look to and see the virtue of hope at work.[4]

I Was Born This Way

Tony Melendez is a Nicaraguan guitar player. This is notable because Tony was born without any arms; he plays guitar with his feet. In 1987, Tony played for St. John Paul II. The pope told Tony, "My wish for you is to continue giving this hope to all, all the people."[5] We cannot help but feel inspired when we see someone overcome a limitation to live a full life. We feel hope that we too might overcome our own hindrances to enjoy a life filled with joy and purpose. Regardless of what others may initially see in us, or even what we see in ourselves, God is able to make the most of what we have to offer.

Practicing the Virtue of Hope

Watch What We Communicate

Be hopeful as you talk to others. Over the years I have occasionally been inwardly convicted of complaining to others at work—"howling at the moon," so to speak. I have been convicted because I am aware of others who use their voice to whisper malice in everyone's ears, and I do not want to be that person. When I can't work up the will to use hopeful language, I must consciously choose to say nothing rather than be negative.

Fight For It

Some of my favorite movies include *The Outlaw Josey Wales*, *Gladiator*, *Jeremiah Johnson*, and *The Last Samurai*. These are great "guy movies," and there is a similar thread that runs through each of them: a man wanting to live in peace is wronged; peace is taken away from him, dragging him into a fight to make things right. These particular movies I mentioned are not spiritual, but there is a bit of hope in them in that the main character is able to endure hardship without being crushed into nothingness by it. Hope is available by standing up, fighting, and finding a way to transcend inescapable suffering. To practice hope like this, we must choose it daily. We must fight and choose to hope in God's promises. We must hope in God when our children start using drugs. We must hope in God when we lose our job or our spouse gets cancer. When difficulties come—and they will—try, fight to be hopeful in it. The reality of heaven and eternal life are not lessened because we have struggles. They exist and will exist forever. Hold onto that promise.

Be Not Afraid

Our society today is rather pessimistic, equating cynicism with realism and disregarding the hopeful optimist as naïve. Many people in our communities are reluctant to embrace hopefulness, afraid that the world won't get any better or that a real tragedy could strike them at any moment. Perhaps this is a fear you share. But circumstances getting worse isn't a sign of misguided hope. No matter the trials coming your way, you can put your hope in God, who is truly constant and ready to help you lead a confident, hopeful life. "Fear not," said the angel to Mary and to the shepherds keeping their sheep. The same is being said to you: Ignore the cynics in society. Fear not. Be optimistic. Have hope.

Catholic Bushido

We alone are responsible for our attitude and for allowing hope the room to grow in our lives. Terrible and negative things happen and have happened to many of us. We may be tempted to trade hope for security, shutting ourselves off from the life God intends for us and isolating ourselves from the community God has given to support us. In the name of self-preservation, we miss out on God's blessings. It takes great courage to set aside our tragic crutches. But when we do, we can become the strongest and most impactful men in our communities. Be courageous. The Dutch priest Henri Nouwen wrote a book called *The Wounded Healer.*[6] This provocative title signifies that our pain and loss equip us to bring relief to those experiencing similar difficulties. In this most mysterious of ways, as Jesus turned water into wine, God can transform our tragedy into a source of healing for others in need.

Prayer

Rise up, O child of God; raise your face to the sun and your hands to heaven. Be warmed for this moment and only this moment, knowing that your Father in heaven has sent this sliver of clarity and warmth to you as a sign, as His smile, as His call and reminder that goodness exists today and forever. Never to be defeated. The joy and happiness of truth is His and now yours because of Christ's great love and sacrifice. Don't cling to, but gently remember this moment. It is your hope.

Scripture for Reflection

"For in hope we were saved. Now hope that sees for itself is not hope. For who hopes for what one sees? But if we hope for what we do not see, we wait with endurance." —Romans 8:24–25

"Blessed be the God and Father of our Lord Jesus Christ, who in his great mercy gave us a new birth to a living hope through the resurrection of Jesus Christ from the dead."

—1 Peter 1:3

"For I know well the plans I have in mind for you—oracle of the LORD— plans for your welfare and not for woe, so as to give you a future of hope."

—Jeremiah 29:11

"But when the kindness and generous love of God our savior appeared, not because of any righteous deeds we had done but because of his mercy, he saved us through the bath of rebirth and renewal by the holy Spirit, whom he richly poured out on us through Jesus Christ our savior, so that we might be justified by his grace and become heirs in hope of eternal life."

—Titus 3:4–7

"Therefore, we are not discouraged; rather, although our outer self is wasting away, our inner self is being renewed day by day. For this momentary light affliction is producing for us an eternal weight of glory beyond all comparison, as we look not to what is seen but to what is unseen; for what is seen is transitory, but what is unseen is eternal."

—2 Corinthians 4:16–18

"May the God of hope fill you with all joy and peace in believing, so that you may abound in hope by the power of the holy Spirit."

—Romans 15:13

Wisdom of the Saints

"Wait upon the Lord; be faithful to His commandments: He will elevate your hope and put you in possession of His kingdom. Wait upon Him patiently: wait upon Him by avoiding all sin. He will come, doubt it not: and in the approaching day of His visitation, which will be that of your death and His judgement, He will Himself crown your holy hope. Place all your hope in the heart of Jesus; it is a safe asylum; for he who trusts in God is sheltered and protected by His mercy. To this firm hope, join the practice of virtue, and even in this life you will begin to taste the ineffable joys of paradise."

—St. Bernard of Clairvaux[7]

"The more a person loves God, the more reason he has to hope in Him. This hope produces in the Saints an unutterable peace, which they preserve even in adversity, because as they love God, and know how beautiful He is to those who love Him, they place all their confidence and find all their repose in Him alone."

—St. Alphonsus Liguori[8]

Questions for Reflection

1. How is hope defined? Is it a soft and gushy emotional response?
2. Is the theological virtue of hope the same as having an attitude of hopefulness? How are they similar, and how are they different?

3. How can hope impact your practice of prudence, fortitude, justice, and temperance?

4. How can you encourage hopefulness in yourself and in others?

5. Can you think of any biblical figures or saints that were hopeful? Name them and explain why they qualify.

9

Love

It's About Us

My eyes turn to heaven.

What pours out of me without words

> *is the breath, the life, the love You have put into me.*

I long for You painfully, with no way of knowing if I will ever attain You.

And still, this outpouring brings me peace,

> *and I wish it would remain this way forever.*

I want it to last because my spirit senses that this love is the sacrifice

> *You desire of me.*

It is at this moment that I am in right relation to You, my God.

Now I worship in truth, on the holy mountain.

I recognize You as the Alpha and the Omega,

　　　　the beginning and the end.

You, Lord God, rightly deserve my praise and my worship.

You, the Creator outside of space and outside of time,

　　　　are all powerful and all good.

I am the lowly creation who, by your grace, can be called your son.

You reach out and lift my chin so I may look at You and be loved.

The *Catechism of the Catholic Church* defines charity (also known as love) as "the theological virtue by which we love God above all things for His own sake, and our neighbor as ourselves for the love of God. It is the form of all the virtues and binds everything together in perfect harmony."[1] This primary virtue inspires and fulfills our most intimate relationships with God and with our fellow man. Our lives find their meaning within these loving relationships. Love enables us to engage in relationships in a right and proper way. As a sinful people, however, we tend to treat relationships as transactional, looking for how we can benefit from our alliances. We need to learn how to respond to and love God and our brothers and sisters for their own sake, for who they are; this is not something we immediately know how to do. So, like all of the theological virtues, love is not attained by our own effort. We receive it when God first pours His love into us.

Be Primitive and Love God

In order to be more open to God's infusing grace, it helps to know and accept our right relationship to Him. So, be primitive. Dance around a bonfire, cook meat over an open flame, skip today's shower, and stay outside all day long. Let's do whatever it takes for us to get over our modern selves and relieve us of our own self-importance. Let's lose this modern-day fantasy that we are so much better than our predecessors. Granted, we have surely excelled in the creation of machinery to extend our lifespans and make our tasks easier. We have spent billions of dollars and man-hours developing technology that helps us understand the world around us in such areas as medicine, microbiology, and astronomy. These things are good.

But they have not kept us from hating, enslaving, and injuring one another. Technology and data generation does not make us wiser or more loving. To grow in love for God, we must grow in humility and have the right attitude.

Primitive people heard thunder, saw lightning, and were awed by its power. They didn't understand its source, but they knew it had nothing to do with their actions. Now that our scientists can look at a lightning strike and provide a detailed analysis of it, is it any less awe-inspiring? Even with all our scientific understanding and mathematical equations, we can describe the power of lightning, but we cannot create a lightning storm. Our analysis and explanations do not contain the created essence of a thing or event. Like a mirror, all we do with words or theories is reflect back what already exists. Even the simulation of a lightning strike in a laboratory is only a copy of what already is. This brings us back again to *Fides et ratio*, St. Pope John Paul II's encyclical on faith and reason, the two ways of knowing.[2] As we strive to know God through faith, and even as we joyfully acknowledge His love, we must also have a right fear (or awe) of Him. The author of the Book of Proverbs says that fear of the Lord is the beginning of wisdom (Proverbs 9:10). This means you must first acknowledge God and then accept that He is greater than you are. Be primitive, leave your own sense of self-importance behind, and fear the Lord; this leads you to your right place before God, where love for Him can blossom.

My Right Relation to God

The papal encyclicals, the church, and the writings of the saints all teach the importance of doing all things for God. "God Alone" is even written in stone above the entryway to the cloister at the Abbey of Gethsemani in Kentucky. Love for God is central to *The Story of a Soul*, the autobiography of St. Therese of Lisieux, the Little Flower.[3] Her childlike, boundless love for God permeated everything she did. She allowed her love for God to flow into every encounter and relationship she had, even when some members of her order were not as charitable. When I observe her "little way" of focusing loving attention on the small things of daily living and in personally being small for God, I have hope. We can all choose to be small. With a simple heart, we can demonstrate love in a small word, a touch, an apology, or in our refusal to angrily respond. Patiently, lightly, and without hurry, we can do all things for God, refusing to count the cost or keep score. This total self-giving to God is difficult to grasp. Even the word *grasp* is not the right one because it gives the idea of control. We don't grasp this love as much as it brushes against us like a curtain blowing in the wind. This love is designed to blow through our lives freely, without predetermined limits on its amount or on the worthiness of those to whom we show it. This love is the free response of a soul that has set everything else aside and completely emptied itself in order to be a useful vessel.

Early on in my own spiritual journey, there were short periods of time in my life where I felt great love for God. But these feelings refused to linger for long. My problem was not a lack of intellectual understanding, and certainly God wasn't changing. The sporadic nature of my love for God was my own fault; I would get too busy thinking about other things in my life and forget about God. By forgetting Him, He was no longer my first priority; something else had replaced Him. Brother Laurence, author of *Practicing the Presence of God,* encouraged his readers not to forget God but to think of Him always.[4] Instead, like the apostles who fell asleep in the garden, I periodically fell asleep to the reality and simplicity of loving God. Because of my clouded perception, I would stop thinking of God as a Father, the Creator who existed before time and space. I was not recognizing or accepting my right place as a created child before the infinite God. By turning away toward something else, I was making that distraction more important than God. My own interests received too much attention. I was not staying small and *allowing* His Spirit to penetrate into the deep parts of my being to show me how He and I were to relate to one another.

But this all changed. I am not sure how God worked this change in me, but I certainly didn't do it on my own. I did not come to a proper perspective through study or deep thinking. But I did pray. I prayed that I could love God as He deserves—that I could *do* this in an active sense. Instead of just feeling love for Him, I wanted to love Him daily through every action I took, through every word I said (and did not say). Although I prayed that God would help me to take action, the first thing God did was direct me into silence and solitude at the Abbey of the Genesee in Piffard, New York. He inclined my heart and mind to pray for the ability to listen. It was there that my heart and spirit unclenched as I disconnected from the noise that surrounded me. The world's intrusions stopped for a few days; in the silence, His ray of love penetrated my heart. Finally I *knew* and felt my right relation to Him. Set free, I loved God freely.

This truth that I experienced reminds me of the words of St. Teresa of Avila. As a college student, I studied her writings, along with some of the works of St. John of the Cross, in my Spanish literature classes. Saint Teresa wrote of "the Transverberation," or piercing of her heart. In one passage, she describes a vision she received of an angel: "I saw in his hand a long spear of gold and at the iron's point there seemed to be a little fire. He appeared to me to be thrusting it at times into my heart...and to leave me all on fire with a great love for God."[5]

The words are beautiful, even poetic, and they speak of divine union with God. However, like the Song of Songs or the writings of St. John of the Cross, her words only just begin to unveil the reality of an unhindered love for God.

Our human language never fully captures the experience of being loved by God. There are no words to contain Him. How can finite words capture the infinite? These figurative descriptions are the best we can manage: God's love is piercing, causing us to cry out in sweet relief. His love simultaneously satisfies and deepens our longing for His presence and His peace. In this piercing is the sweet and blissful feeling of completion, of being filled and made whole, all while being poured out and emptied through love to act, praise, and worship Him. This filling and emptying at the same time is God's gift to us.

These words about love and piercing and awe may sound strange. To some men they may even sound weak or feminine, but we must reject any false pride that might prevent us from submitting to the love of God. God wants all people to know that He is real and that His love for us is real. He wants us to know that there is hope and that He deeply desires a relationship with us. That there is a love and a hope that surpass any words we can ever use. The sweetest love you will ever know is calling out to you today. Calling you to come home. The Father is waiting to kill the fattened calf and to put rings on your fingers. **And when He sees you turn**, He will hike up His robes and sprint down the road to meet you, and He will hold you close, and you will love Him and be complete. Here, at this moment of mutual embrace, we are in right relation to our God.

What Is Love?

We often casually say things like "I love this black raspberry pie" or "I love the *Lord of the Rings* movies." These are just words. We use the word *love* too freely and a little too often. We use it to describe the feeling of momentary pleasures derived from food, movies, shoes, sex, jokes, or the color of painted walls. We're describing a preference rather than something that animates and elevates our very being. If we live our lives consciously, however, our understanding of love matures and is transformed over time. This occurs because our life experiences with other people *cause* it to change.

When I was young, I loved others because of what I received in return. This love was not just selfish, it was insecure. Love is insecure when it is motivated by the selfish pursuit of one's own pleasure and happiness while fearing its loss. Getting married and having children deepened my maturity and my understanding of love. I had no choice but to grow. I learned to give more, to sacrifice for the sake of my wife and my sons. I didn't and still don't do it perfectly, but I have moved in that direction by the grace of God.

Because of new relationships and an awareness of the experiences of life, love develops. With God's grace, love becomes more like what St. Paul exhorted us to:

> "Love is patient, love is kind. It is not jealous, [love] is not pompous, it is not inflated, it is not rude, it does not seek its own interests, it is not quick-tempered, it does not brood over injury, it does not rejoice over wrongdoing but rejoices with the truth. It bears all things, believes all

things, hopes all things, endures all things. Love never fails" (1 Corinthians 13:4–8).

Love, then, is not a preference or a way of acting, but it flows through everything we do; it is a way of being.

In trying to understand the nature of love as a way of being, consider Pope Benedict XVI's encyclical *Deus caritas est*, "God is Love."[6] He does not say that God loves but that He **is** love—He is love's very essence. How lucky are we that this is our God? The God who *is* love has called us to be like Himself. We are called to imitate Christ by allowing His Spirit to fully work through our humanity in charity. This is who we are called to be, and this is what makes us whole and complete. But we cannot achieve this way of being in an instant. Nor will we ever reach a "satisfactory level" of loving. By God's grace acting in us, the transformation never stops. It continues on slowly and quietly as we journey through our lives. Our job is to permit God's grace to do its work. We must surrender and die to ourselves daily, giving God's love free reign to work in us.

Examples of Charity

The Trappist Monks of The Abbey of the Genesee

I admire the Catholic priesthood and all members of religious orders (male and female) who profess vows and "give up" marriage, sexual relations, home ownership, and other things we in the laity consider "normal." I have an outsider's perspective, but I can't imagine anything other than love could motivate someone to choose such a life. These monks are driven by love of God and love of neighbor. Consecrated life, in all of its forms, is the exchange of earthly things for heavenly treasures, choosing a life of service to God and His people.

I believe we should appreciate the example provided to us by these men and women and show them our love. And so each summer I accompany a group of men on a five-hour trek to the Abbey of the Genesee in Piffard, New York. I have been going there for over a dozen years now. These Trappist monks have meant so much to me on my spiritual journey. As I have interacted with them over the years, the one thing that stands out is something that I sense rather than see, hear, touch, or smell. I sense and experience a great peace and love that flows out from these men. From the moment I met them, I knew instantly that they loved God and loved me. I am very thankful for them.

Billy Graham

It is estimated that Billy Graham, in his lifetime, preached to over 200 million people.[7] Considering that today's population of the United States is just over 320 million, this is an astounding number. Billy Graham dedicated his life to preaching the gospel of salvation in Jesus Christ. To preach salvation is to love people, to be grieved by their separation from God. When I attended one of Billy Graham's crusades as I described earlier, something that stood out to me during this event is that he welcomed Catholics to join him on stage and to work with him at his crusades. Driven by love of God and neighbor, Billy Graham spent his life preaching around the world while rejecting the anti-Catholic bias that plagues many Protestant churches today. The focus was love of God and neighbor.

Mother Teresa

I can think of no greater example of the virtue of love than St. Teresa of Calcutta. This small, frail lady is my hero. She heard her "call within a call" and **left everything**! She moved into the slums of India to serve the poorest of the poor. Sitting here in the United States, I really have no comprehension of her sacrifice. The sick and impoverished people of India and the conditions in which they live are as foreign to me as the living conditions on Mars. But St. Teresa persevered in her loving service. For the last 35 years of her life, her spiritual life was very dry, dark, and without consolation. But she continued on with her work to serve God by caring for these poor people. This is love lived in a way that I deeply admire. I am so thankful for her inspirational life. I am thankful to Jesus that He sent St. Teresa of Calcutta to demonstrate for us what we can do in Him. This to me is one of the reasons we have the saints. They are all human beings who lived in an extraordinary fashion. Their path is open to us as well by living in the way chosen for us by our heavenly Father, every act inspired by love.

St. Joseph Cares

Our local parish has an outreach group of about eight to ten people who focus on helping those in need. The group's mission statement is pretty simple: to serve people by following the corporal and spiritual works of mercy. Members of this group distribute emergency funds to those who need help paying for food, water, utilities, or rent. Additionally, members of this group write notes to the people on the parish's prayer list, play bingo at a local nursing home once a month, collect and distribute clothes at a local community center, disseminate information concerning drug addiction, and send letters and gifts to parishioners on active duty in the U.S. military. This group is inspired to be the loving hands and feet of Christ bringing a small bit of relief and peace to people in the local community. This nudge that encourages us to move out in small ways and bring healing to a stranger is motivated by the virtue of charity.

Charity can be as big as St. Teresa of Calcutta's life work and as simple as local parishioners providing help and relief to their community. God's love flows throughout the world continuously. This love moves in quiet ways, imperceptible to all but those directly touched. But it is there in overwhelming abundance and with an enduring strength that brings us all great joy, confidence, and hope.

Cultivating Love

Practice Silence in Solitude

In our world we have many distractions that keep us from anything but superficial thoughts and concepts—Twitter being a prime example. There is a remedy, however. I mentioned previously my annual retreats to a monastery. This time in silence helps to bring things back into balance. These retreats have provided me with many of the most profound spiritual experiences of my life in which I have been acutely aware of God's presence. But even in our customary places, we can pursue silence. It requires us to turn off devices, quiet our chatty brains, and just sit and *be* for a moment. In these times of simplicity—silent, with an open heart—God can be heard. Remember, He is not in the earthquake but in the whisper.

Pray

To cultivate love in my personal prayer life, first I need to get down to the most basic level and pray that I might believe more fully. I need to believe that God is there, to really know it every minute of every day. I do know that God exists because of the ways He has worked and moved in the events of my life, but sometimes in my human day-to-day weakness, my memory of His presence fades.

I start with belief, then I pray for the grace to acknowledge my right relation to Him. I want to consciously consider the infinite nature of God. God is the Creator of *all* space and time. He exists outside of it—not just the "physical" sense of outside, but He is not bound by space or time. God is. And His love and care exist for me and for all of creation. I am not the center of existence—God is, and I merely have a part to play. My role is important and completely fulfills my life.

So I pray first that I might believe, then that I might recognize my place relative to God's, and finally I pray that I might love God as He desires and as He deserves. His love for me is perfect, even though I really don't comprehend what perfect means. God is love, and the only adequate response to love is love in return. This is the path of perfection. Love, and specifically love for God. I believe that if I love God first and rightly, then loving other people will just happen naturally.

Willfully Take Steps to Draw Near to God

Knowing God will help us to draw nearer to Him. One way to do this is to read Scripture daily. During certain stretches of time, I will read the daily Mass readings, along with a written reflection on them. Other times I will take a book of the Bible and read a chapter a day. I will purposefully strive to take my time and read...and...concentrate...on...each...word. This is how I allow God to get into my head through the Scriptures—by focusing on His words. My intention is to hear the words. Not necessarily to study them with the hope of pulling out some new meaning, but to hear God for the sake of knowing Him.

You should also read other spiritual works by the saints or other Catholic spiritual writers. I believe God has worked through these many different people to plant in us the seeds that will help us to grow into who our Father wants us as individuals to be. Certain writings of one saint and that of another writer will come together to help you on your path.

Go to Mass every week. I guess this could go without saying, but it shouldn't. We receive the body and blood of Christ at every Mass. We are physically joined to Him. I know that I receive grace from this. I also know that in both attending *and* participating in Mass I am participating in the worship of God, which supports my desire to be in right relation to Him. Going to Mass is an outward expression of my love for God.

I also attend men's group meetings at my parish. By taking time to walk alongside my brothers in Christ, I learn much more about the full face of God. He shows Himself to my brothers in ways that are not necessarily how He shows Himself to me, and this new perspective helps me to know God better. God also uses these times to confirm, or in some cases correct, my thoughts and feelings about certain situations.

Sacrifice Your Time for Something Bigger than You

This does not have to be burdensome, but just take the small step of giving yourself (not just money) to the parish and larger community. Whenever we sacrifice in our family relationships, we know that we "get" something in return, such as peace in our home. But when we sacrifice and give for the community, there is a very good possibility that we will get nothing in return—or at least there is no expectation for repayment. The funny and secret thing is by cultivating our love in this way, we still end up receiving abundance in return.

We must strive to look outside of ourselves and see our world as clearly and honestly as we can. Let's try to see it for what it is through the eyes of Christ. Let's see the beggar or homeless man on the street. Let's look at him, make eye contact, and not look away. Can you say ten words to him? Walk into a nursing home with no one specific to visit. Find someone to sit with for five minutes. Ask the nurses; they'll tell you who gets company and who doesn't. Take your children with you when you do it. Consider coaching a youth team and purposefully care about all of the kids. Help them to grow and become more confident. Let's be salt and light in our homes and in our neighborhoods. This is love in action. We can do it; we were made for this. We were made for one another.

Catholic Bushido

As Catholic warriors, we are challenged to love and love rightly. We must love our wives, our sons, our daughters, our parents, brothers and sisters, friends and neighbors. We must be different, and those people in our lives must know it, sense it, and see it clearly. It is up to us to lead in this way. No one else will do it for us. Plow the field of your own soul so that when God, in His grace, plants seeds of love, they will have space to grow. Be godly men; surrender to God's will and lead in love.

Prayer

Lord God in heaven, my Creator and my Father, help me. I do all things imperfectly, most of all loving You. Please Lord, help me to get out of

Your way. Let me silently and simply let go of what I believe to be important. May I see that the only important thing is to be an empty and cracked vessel that Your goodness and love can flow through freely. May I love you as a child would: simply, honestly, and freely. May my love for You animate all that I do, and may I give love freely to my brothers and sisters. In Jesus' holy name, I pray. Amen.

Scripture for Reflection

"Jesus replied, 'The first is this: "Hear, O Israel! The Lord our God is Lord alone! You shall love the Lord your God with all your heart, with all your soul, with all your mind, and with all your strength." The second is this: "You shall love your neighbor as yourself." There is no other commandment greater than these.'"

—Mark 12:29–31

"When I was a child, I used to talk as a child, think as a child, reason as a child; when I became a man, I put aside childish things. At present we see indistinctly, as in a mirror, but then face to face. At present I know partially; then I shall know fully, as I am fully known. So, faith, hope, love remain, these three; but the greatest of these is love."

—1 Corinthians 13:11–13

"And over all these put on love, that is, the bond of perfection."

—Colossians 3:14

"Beloved, let us love one another, because love is of God; everyone who loves is begotten by God and knows God. Whoever is without love does not know God, for God is love."

—*1 John 4:7–8*

"I, then, a prisoner for the Lord, urge you to live in a manner worthy of the call you have received, with all humility and gentleness, with patience, bearing with one another through love, striving to preserve the unity of the spirit through the bond of peace."

—*Ephesians 4:1–3*

"Above all, let your love for one another be intense, because love covers a multitude of sins."

—*1 Peter 4:8*

Wisdom of the Saints

"Helping a person in need is good in itself. But the degree of goodness is hugely affected by the attitude with which it is done. If you show resentment because you are helping the person out of a reluctant sense of duty, then the person may receive your help but may feel awkward and embarrassed. This is because he will feel beholden to you. If, on the other hand, you help the person in a spirit of joy, then the help will be received joyfully. The person will feel neither demeaned nor humiliated by your help, but rather will feel glad to have caused you pleasure by receiving your help. And joy is the appropriate attitude with which to help others because acts of generosity are a source of blessing to the giver as well as the receiver."

—*St. John Chrysostom*[8]

"Do not think that love in order to be genuine has to be extraordinary. What we need is to love without getting tired. Be faithful in small things because it is in them that your strength lies."

—*St. Teresa of Calcutta*[9]

"The greatest disease in the West today is not TB or leprosy; it is being unwanted, unloved, and uncared for. We can cure physical diseases with medicine, but the only cure for loneliness, despair, and hopelessness is love. There are many in the world who are dying for a piece of bread but there are many more dying for a little love. The poverty in the West is a different kind of poverty—it is not only a poverty of loneliness but also of spirituality. There's a hunger for love, as there is a hunger for God."

—*St. Teresa of Calcutta*[10]

"One cannot love unless it is at their own expense."

—*St. Teresa of Calcutta*[11]

Questions for Reflection

1. Is love an emotion, an act of the will, or a grace from God? Explain.

2. How is understanding your right relation to God related to your love for Him?

3. What are some ways in which you can be open to allowing God's grace to work in you, growing your love for Him and others?

4. Can you think of anything more important than love? How does love flow into, flow through, and support all of the other virtues?

5. How can you know more personally that God truly loves you?

10

Catholic Bushido

The Way of the Catholic Warrior

"Do not conform yourself to this age but be transformed by the renewal of your mind, that you may discern what is the will of God, what is good and pleasing and perfect."

—*Romans 12:2*

When the book of Romans was written, St. Paul's readers were living in one particular "age," and today we are living in an "age" that is different in many ways. In our modern, technologically advanced age, we have very specific advantages, challenges, and shortcomings, some of which are brand new to humanity—but what holds true across the millennia, from Saint Paul's time to ours today, is our struggle to resist the attraction of vice. Just as in St. Paul's day, we are confronted with temptation and with a culture that encourages us to think and act selfishly and in ways contrary to God's perfect will. And human nature is likewise the same as it ever was: we're all too willing to give in to desire and go along with the prevailing whims of the age.

Truth be told, however, as persuasive as the crowd can be, it is not society's fault that we sin, falling short of who and what God has created us to be. It is our own fault, no one else's. We may be tempted by our culture's offerings, and it is true that we can be greatly impacted by our family and environment. But you and I have been given a great gift: free will. We can choose for ourselves. In the grander scheme of things, this is really all that we can do. We choose. In one sense, your life could be described as just a long list of choices you make and their resulting consequences. The hopeful point here is that the very next choice you make could actually be the one that turns your life around and brings you years of great joy and peace. For good or ill, free will empowers the slow and imperceptible forces of transformation in your life. For this transformation to be good, you need direction and guidance that comes from God through His Holy Spirit and the church.

Transformation is a long-term process, not an event. We can appreciate this by looking at our world around us, at the wonders of nature. Watch any time-lapse video of plants growing, flowers opening, or even a butterfly escaping its cocoon, and you'll see a process. The process is so exceedingly gradual that time must be sped up for us to "see" it happen. We should also note that the transformation process is marked by struggle and difficulty. The butterfly's escape from its cocoon seems arduous, possibly painful to our eyes, as does the plant breaking out from its seed. The buildup of strength, through struggle, seems to be a part of all positive transformation. Just ask the professional athlete who lives in a nearly constant state of training. Becoming something new and good—going from a place of negativity, pain, and despair to one of joy and peace—is not easy. But as Catholic Christian men, we are called to choose this transformation, not to be stopped by the world, this age, and its difficulties.

So transformation is a slow process. One that may include struggles and pain. This can seem overwhelming and none too attractive for many of us. "A long-term painful struggle? Where do I sign up?" said no one, ever! We must recognize that one of the key de-motivators that our enemy slips into our mind is impatience. God is eternally patient, but the devil makes us think that we must be perfected *now*. That's neither true nor possible. I believe that all God asks is that we walk the path faithfully. This is not a cop-out but an honest challenge; we must put effort into walking the path. Because when we do, we'll be doing our best to walk with God. And that is what He wants. The impatience the devil pushes on us is fueled by our American ideal of success as an end point. But we have no spiritual end point while here on this earth. Instead of becoming frustrated by our cultural trappings, we should joyfully accept our freedom. We can be free of the impatient expectation of spiritual success. We are free to walk with God and to desire our spiritual transformation in Him, without placing boundaries on what that might look like. God is ready to move in the silent spaces outside of our busy and noisy lives, and His movement is never-ending. His acts of creation and redemption are constantly at work in our lives and in the world, even when we are completely unaware. The path of change and transformation only requires that we take one step, then another, patiently, faithfully, and without expectation of what or where we should be.

Transformational Virtue

Taking steps without knowing the destination is not easy for us. This is where the virtues come in; they are the beacon light of "how." The virtues do not tell you what you will become or show you where you will end up. But they are like the breadcrumbs on the trail directly in front of you. They show you enough for the next step, no more. By patiently, simply, and without anxiety practicing the virtues, your spirit will slow down and become more disposed to hearing or sensing the nudging of the Holy Spirit. It is all still God's grace, His plan, and His purpose that guide everything. Our role is to stay close to the path, prepared to receive. We must be like the virgins with the oil lamps waiting for the bridegroom to come (Matthew 25:1–13).

Example of Transformation

St. Augustine of Hippo

The *Confessions* of St. Augustine are just that. The book is the story of a highly intelligent man who led a life of debauchery in his younger days. This lifestyle continued until one day Augustine heard a voice calling out to him to "take and read." In response to this calling, he opened the Bible and read a section from Romans 13 that condemned many of the earthly activities he was engaging in. Augustine converted and was baptized. From this point forward, his transformation included becoming a priest, then a bishop, and ultimately he was named a Doctor of the Church. The transformation of St. Augustine continued on. It did not end when he turned from his sinful ways or when he became a priest or bishop. We focus on these events in the lives of people, but we know that it is the daily obedience of a person's faith that causes him to grow in God's grace. My favorite quote by St. Augustine says, "Thou hast made us for thyself, O Lord, and our heart is restless until it finds rest in thee."[1] Holy Spirit–infused restlessness makes us move, and this movement can become transformation.

The Gold Coats

More than two decades ago at the California Men's Colony, a medium-security prison in Southern California, a new program assigned high-functioning inmates as caregivers for some of the less abled members of the prison population. These caregiver men wore gold coats over their standard prison uniforms. They got up each morning and assisted those inmates who needed help eating, getting washed and dressed, and going to their daily appointments in the prison. This program continues today.

Dr. Cheryl Steed is a senior psychologist specialist at the prison. All of the Gold Coats she works with are incarcerated for murder. So here are these men who have committed very serious crimes, who have hurt people as badly as you can—yet now, some years later, they are helping an incontinent elderly man get himself cleaned up if he has an accident. For many of these men, their inspiration initially came from a desire to atone for their crimes, but through this process of caring for another person, they learn empathy and kindness. They themselves are transformed. They are not the same men who entered the prison.[2]

Jacques Fesch

Jacques Fesch grew up in a very unhappy home and never really found his way in society. His girlfriend became pregnant with his child and, soon after, they were married in a civil ceremony. The addition of a wife and child did nothing to ward off his unhappiness, so finally Jacques deserted them both. His hunt for happiness morphed into an obsessive idea to buy a yacht and sail to Polynesia. Unfortunately for Fesch, he had no money, and his parents would not loan him the needed amount. This led him to commit burglary; as he made his escape, he shot and killed a police officer. He was caught, put into prison, and sentenced to death. Fesch had no faith growing up, but while in prison he read a book about Our Lady. Over time he was transformed, developing a deep and true prayer life. Because he was in solitary confinement, his cell became for him a cloister. He wrote many letters to his wife about his transformation. Intrigued, she began to visit him in prison. Fesch's expressions of his faith had a deep impact on his wife's spiritual journey. In the end Jacques was executed for his crimes, but his writings continue to inspire people throughout the world. A model for the redemptive potential of faith in God, he has now been put forward for beatification. Transformation can happen anywhere, even alone in a jail cell.[3]

Thomas Merton

Thomas Merton was a Trappist monk, an author, and a teacher. He wrote over sixty books and multiple volumes of poetry, articles, and drawings. He died in 1968. Like St. Augustine, Thomas Merton lived a free-spirited life of drinking and self-indulgence as a young man. Following his spiritual awakening, Thomas Merton was baptized, joined a religious order, and wrote prodigiously. He has since touched and encouraged millions of Catholic Christians. Here again we see how the transformation process continues for a lifetime. His autobiography *The Seven Story Mountain* is truly required reading for anyone looking for hope in conversion.[4]

My Father

While my father was an alcoholic, so was his brother, his father before him, and so on. My dad also had a lot of goodness inside of him. He had a real heart for the poor and less fortunate. I remember him having our family take part in a program that had disadvantaged inner-city kids come live at our home for a week. This program was intended to give these young men a different kind of vision for their lives. My father also invited other people to come live in our home, including friends of my brothers and an older lady from our parish. He loved to open our house to people. That's why it is not surprising that he tried to stop drinking.

He was "on the wagon" for four to five years. During this time he practiced temperance by choosing not to drink at all. He completely stopped and was transformed; I was proud of him, and there was peace between us and within our family. While he was sober, he attended AA meetings and became a sponsor to a young African-American man from the inner city who had small children. My dad tried to help this man and his family, even employing the man for a while in the company he ran. But then for whatever reason, my dad ended up falling off the wagon and started drinking again. He continued drinking from that point until the day he died.

Transformation, once achieved, is not final. The danger of regression or falling away will always be with us. We must exercise constant vigilance and practice virtue until we reach our eternal reward with God in heaven.

Transforming for Others

When I was a young man, I also drank alcohol, and many times to excess. Although I never fell into the constant, daily drinking of an alcoholic nor lacked the ability to stop, I sensed a desire for drinking inside of me. I liked it.

After my sons were born and while they were both still very young, my wife Angela and I had an experience of God speaking to our hearts. We were on a car ride to do some shopping and were talking about my dad and other family situations. At that moment, God separately spoke into both of our hearts the message that I needed to stop drinking alcohol for the sake of my sons and to break the chain of addiction. We did not immediately share this with each other, but in this revelation, the "good" was clearly set before me, as was the sacrifice I would have to make. In the days that followed, I continued to think about this moment of inspiration, wondering if I would indeed follow this call to stop drinking.

Sometime later I shared this deliberation with my sister, describing the way that God spoke to me. Unbeknownst to me, my wife had already had a conversation with my sister and told her the message she had received from God. So my sister then shared with me what my wife had told her. As soon as I got off the phone with my sister, my wife and I had an amazing discussion about this, marveling at how God reveals truth to us so clearly sometimes. She told me the message she had received, and for me there was no more need for deliberation. It was clear that the Holy Spirit was working. I stopped drinking alcohol and have not had a drink in over fifteen years.

In this case of prudential living, the good was shown to me, I thought about the choice, sought counsel with my wife, and acted. I have no doubt that this was the right thing for me to do for my marriage, for my sons, and for their future families. I know this without question. This decision to stop drinking has transformed my life and brought me a freedom that I did not know I needed. I realize now there was a fear tucked into the back of my consciousness about alcoholism in my family and in my life, and I am now completely free of that.

Catholic Bushido

The *Catechism of the Catholic Church* says that the seven gifts of the Holy Spirit complete and perfect the virtues of those who receive them. They make the faithful docile in readily obeying divine inspirations. These gifts are wisdom, understanding, counsel, fortitude, knowledge, piety, and fear of the Lord. We must pray for these gifts constantly.

Men of God, we are called to daily surrender. Our role is to live each day deliberately and to lead our families with virtue and integrity. It takes discipline to do this—it takes practice and the will to never give up. We will fail, we will be challenged, but we are called to rise up and continue moving forward.

Rise up, men of God! Let go of the things that inhibit your outward love for God. Be salt and light to the world. Be salt and light to your family, your wife, your sons, your daughters, your friends—everyone you meet. No one else can do the job you were specially made for. God has given you everything that you need to accomplish it. You are created, called, prepared, and strengthened for what it is you must do. Do not be afraid. Move forward into the unknown places and make your home there. The Lord your God is with you!

Prayer

O mighty and loving God. Thank You. Thank You for the hope that You infuse into us, the hope that bursts out into joy. May we be men who are strong and courageous enough to surrender to You. May we lay aside our selfish desires while picking up Your standard and carrying it into our daily battle. Give us the wisdom we need so that we know when to speak and when to stay quiet, when to charge and when to set up our defenses. Be our General, Lord God, so that all things may be done as You will and not as we think or desire. Amen.

Scriptures for Reflection

"To this day, in fact, whenever Moses is read, a veil lies over their hearts, but whenever a person turns to the Lord the veil is removed. Now the Lord is the Spirit, and where the Spirit of the Lord is, there is freedom. All of us, gazing with unveiled face on the glory of the Lord, are being transformed into the same image from glory to glory, as from the Lord who is the Spirit."

—2 Corinthians 3:15–18

"A clean heart create for me, God; renew within me a steadfast spirit."

—Psalm 51:12

"I urge you therefore, brothers, by the mercies of God, to offer your bodies as a living sacrifice, holy and pleasing to God, your spiritual worship. Do not conform yourselves to this age but be transformed by the renewal of your mind, that you may discern what is the will of God, what is good and pleasing and perfect."

—Romans 12:1–2

"I will give you a new heart, and a new spirit I will put within you. I will remove the heart of stone from your flesh and give you a heart of flesh."

—Ezekiel 36:26

"So whoever is in Christ is a new creation: the old things have passed away; behold, new things have come."

—2 Corinthians 5:17

"But when the kindness and generous love of God our savior appeared, not because of any righteous deeds we had done but because of his mercy, he saved us through the bath of rebirth and renewal by the holy Spirit, whom he richly poured out on us through Jesus Christ our savior, so that we might be justified by his grace and become heirs in hope of eternal life."

—Titus 3:4–7

Wisdom of the Saints

"Yet through virtuous living man is further ordained to a higher end, which consists in the enjoyment of God, as we have said above. Consequently, since society must have the same end as the individual man, it is not the ultimate end of an assembled multitude to live virtuously, but through virtuous living to attain to the possession of God."

—*Thomas Aquinas*[5]

"God doesn't require us to succeed, he only requires that you try."

—*St. Teresa of Calcutta*[6]

Questions for Reflection

1. Think of some examples of transformation in the natural world. How rapidly does it happen in most cases?
2. Is spiritual transformation in my life solely dependent on my efforts? Do I have a role to play?
3. How can practicing virtue draw me closer to God? Is it just about me being more virtuous? What does it do to my heart?
4. How can my practice of the virtues impact my family, friends, workplace, and society? Give examples.
5. How can I promote the practicing of virtue to others?

Chapter 1

[1] Marsh, Abigail. "Why Some People Are More Altruistic than Others." *Ted,* June 2016, www.ted.com/talks/abigail_marsh_why_some_people_are_more_altruistic_than_others?language=en. Accessed 27 February 2019.

[2] Dahlsgaard, K., Peterson, C., Seligman, M.E.P. "Shared Virtue: The Convergence of Valued Human Strengths Across Culture and History," *Review of General Psychology*, Vol 9, No 3, 203–213, 2005.

[3] *Catechism of the Catholic Church*, Paragraph 27. Libreria Editrice Vaticana, 1993.

[4] *"virtue" and "vice." Random House Unabridged Dictionary*, 2019.

[5] Aurelius Prudentius Clemens. "The Battle for the Soul of Man (Psychomachia)." web.archive.org/web/20020429135514/http://www.richmond.edu/~wstevens/grvaltexts/psychomachia.html. Accessed 27 February 2019.

[6] *Catechism of the Catholic Church*, Paragraphs 1803–1829. Libreria Editrice Vaticana, 1993.

[7] St. John Chrysostom. *The Homilies of S. John Chrysostom, Archbishop of Constantinople on the Epistle of St. Paul the Apostle to the Romans.* Translated by members of the English Church, Oxford, John Henry Parker, 1848.

[8] St. Ignatius of Loyola. *Thoughts of Ignatius Loyola for Every Day in the Year.* Translated from the *Scintillae Ignatianae* of Father Gabriel Hevenesi, S.J., by Alan McDougall, Burns Oates and Washbourne Ltd., 1928.

[9] St. Padre Pio. www.goodreads.com/quotes/389836-the-life-of-a-christian-is-nothing-but-a-perpetual. Accessed 27 February 2019.

Chapter 2

[1] St. John Cassian. "The Conferences." New York: Newman Press, 1997, pp. 183–196.

[2] *Catechism of the Catholic Church*, Paragraph 1847. Libreria Editrice Vaticana, 1993.

[3] *Catechism of the Catholic Church*, Paragraph 2351. Libreria Editrice Vaticana, 1993.

[4] Bray, G., Macdiarmid, J. "The Epidemic of Obesity." *Western Journal of Medicine*, February 2000, 172(2): 78–79.

[5] Healy, M. "Nearly 4 in 10 US adults now obese, CDC says." *Cleveland Plain Dealer*, 14 October 2017, pp A6.

[6] Suprenant, L.J. "The Sin of Sloth." *Catholic Answers,* 1 January 1 2008.

[7] St. Alphonsus Liguori. "On the Sin of Anger." *The Sermons of St. Alphonsus Liguori,* 1852.

[8] *Catechism of the Catholic Church*, Paragraph 1866. Libreria Editrice Vaticana, 1993.

[9] Aurelius Prudentius Clemens. "The Battle for the Soul of Man (Psychomachia)." web.archive.org/web/20020429135514/http://www.richmond.edu/~wstevens/grvaltexts/psychomachia.html. Accessed 27 February 2019.

[10] St. John Chrysostom. www.goodreads.com/quotes/166476-i-do-not-know-whether-anyone-has-ever-succeeded-in. Accessed 27 February 2019.

Chapter 3

[1] *Catechism of the Catholic Church*, Paragraph 1806. Libreria Editrice Vaticana, 1993.

[2] *Catechism of the Catholic Church*, Paragraph 1806. Libreria Editrice Vaticana, 1993.

[3] St. Joseph Catholic Church, Strongsville, Ohio. "Lesson 27: The Cardinal Virtue of Prudence." sjohio.org/assets/templates/mycustom/ethereal/files/lesson/holyspirit/Lesson27ATheCardinalVirtueof%20Prudence.pdf. Accessed on 27 February 2019.

[4] St. Francis of Assisi. *The Writings of St. Francis of Assisi*. Translated by Paschal Robinson, 1901.

[5] St. Thomas Aquinas. *Summa Theologica.* 1274.

Chapter 4

[1] *Catechism of the Catholic Church*, Paragraph 1807. Libreria Editrice Vaticana, 1993.

[2] Aristotle. "Politics." 328 B.C.

[3] Merton, T. *Conjectures of a Guilty Bystander*. 1966. Image Classic, 2014, p 154.

[4] *Catechism of the Catholic Church*, Paragraph 1928. Libreria Editrice Vaticana, 1993.

[5] St. Francis of Assisi. *The Writings of St. Francis of Assisi*. Translated by Paschal Robinson, 1901.

[6] St. Thomas Aquinas. *Summa Theologica.* 1274.

[7] St. Thomas Aquinas. *Summa Theologica.* 1274.

[8] St. Teresa of Calcutta. "Mother Teresa Reflects on Working Toward Peace." legacy.scu.edu/ethics/architects-of-peace/Teresa/essay.html. Accessed on 27 February 2019.

Chapter 5

[1] *Catechism of the Catholic Church*, Paragraph 1807. Libreria Editrice Vaticana, 1993.

[2] Craig, J. "Made for Greatness?" *Those Catholic Men,* 11 January 2017. thosecatholicmen.com/articles/made-for-greatness/. Accessed on 27 February 2019.

[3] Guardini, R. *Learning the Virtues that Lead You to God*. 1963. Translated by Stella Lange, Henry Regnery Company, 1967. Sophia Institute Press, 1998, p 92.

[4] St. Thomas Aquinas. *Summa Theologica*. 1274.

[5] St. Thomas Aquinas. *Summa Theologica*. 1274.

[6] St. John Chrysostom. *Homilies on the Statutes,* Homily 3. 387.

Chapter 6

[1] *Catechism of the Catholic Church*, Paragraph 1808. Libreria Editrice Vaticana, 1993.

[2] Catechism of the Catholic Church, Paragraph 2515. Libreria Editrice Vaticana, 1993.

[3] Yogis, J., *The Fear Project: What our Most Primal Emotion Taught Me About Survival, Success, Surfing...and Love.* Rodale Books, 2013.

[4] "A Conversation with Dr. Tom Catena." *Catholic Medical Mission Board*, 26 May 2017. cmmb.org/volunteer-blog/conversation-dr-tom-catena/. Accessed on 27 February 2019.

[5] "St. Maximilian Kolbe." *Catholic Online*. www.catholic.org/saints/saint.php?saint_id=370. Accessed on 27 February 2019.

[6] Tolkein, J.R.R. *The Silmarillion*. Ballantine Books, 1982, p 22.

[7] St. Thomas Aquinas. *Summa Theologica*. 1274.

[8] St. Ignatius of Loyola. *Thoughts of Ignatius Loyola for Every Day in the Year.* Translated from the *Scintillae Ignatianae* of Father Gabriel Hevenesi, S.J., by Alan McDougall, Burns Oates and Washbourne Ltd., 1928.

[9] St. Teresa of Calcutta. www.goodreads.com/quotes/288714-a-sacrifice-to-be-real-must-cost-must-hurt-and. Accessed on 27 February 2019.

Chapter 7

[1] St. John Paul II. "Fides et Ratio" (Faith and Reason). 14 September 1998. w2.vatican.va/content/john-paul-ii/en/encyclicals/documents/hf_jp-ii_enc_14091998_fides-et-ratio.html, Chapter 3, paragraph 26. Accessed 27 February 2019.

[2] *Catechism of the Catholic Church*, Paragraph 1266. Libreria Editrice Vaticana, 1993.

[3] *Catechism of the Catholic Church*, Paragraph 1814. Libreria Editrice Vaticana, 1993.

[4] Merton, T. *Thoughts in Solitude*. Farrar, Straus and Giroux, April 2011, p 68.

[5] *Nicene Creed*. www.usccb.org/beliefs-and-teachings/what-we-believe/. Accessed 27 February 2019.

[6] Mother Teresa with Brian Kolodiejchuk. *Mother Teresa; Come Be My Light: The Private Writings of the "Saint of Calcutta."* Doubleday, 2007, p 2.

[7] Springer, R. "Interview with Beth Nimmo." *Risen Magazine*, 20 Oct 2016. http://www.risenmagazine.com/beth-nimmo/. Accessed 27 February 2019.

[8] Barron R. "Catholicism, Episode 1: Amazed and Afraid." *Word on Fire Digital.* www.wofdigital.org/packages/catholicism-series/videos/catholictv-catholicismep1-hd-1080p/. Accessed 27 February 2019.

[9] St. Thomas Aquinas. *Summa Theologica.* 1274.

[10] St. Padre Pio. www.goodreads.com/quotes/1027306-the-most-beautiful-act-of-faith-is-the-one-made. Accessed 27 February 2019.

[11] St. Irenaeus of Lyon. *Against Heresies.* 180. Translated by Alexander Roberts and William Rambaut, 1885.

Chapter 8

[1] *Catechism of the Catholic Church*, Paragraph 1817. Libreria Editrice Vaticana, 1993.

[2] Blenkhorn, A. "Keep On the Sunny Side." 1899.

[3] Frankl, V. *Man's Search for Meaning*. Beacon Press, 2006, p 65.

[4] The Joni and Friends website. www.joniandfriends.org/about/our-history/. Accessed 27 February 2019.

[5] Melendez, T. "Papal Performance." *YouTube,* uploaded by toejammusic on 3 February 2009, www.youtube.com/watch?v=9Xjsr3bNLiM. Accessed 27 February 2019.

[6] Nouwen, H. *The Wounded Healer: Ministry in Contemporary Society.* Doubleday, 1972.

[7] Fenelon, M. "Ten Quotes about Hope to Lift Your Spirits." *Marge Steinhage Fenelon*, 25 October 2012, margefenelon.com/1870/ten-quotes-about-hope-to-lift-your-spirits/. Accessed 27 February 2019.

[8] St. Alphonsus Liguori. *The Love of Our Lord Jesus Christ Reduced to Practice.* Translated in 1841.

Chapter 9

[1] *Catechism of the Catholic Church*, Paragraph 1822–1829. Libreria Editrice Vaticana, 1993.

[2] St. John Paul II. "Fides et Ratio" (Faith and Reason). 14 September 1998. w2.vatican.va/content/john-paul-ii/en/encyclicals/documents/hf_jp-ii_enc_14091998_fides-et-ratio.html, Chapter 3, paragraph 26. Accessed 27 February 2019.

[3] St. Therese of Lisieux. *The Story of a Soul.* 1898.

[4] Brother Lawrence. *The Practice of the Presence of God*. Ichthus Publications, 2015.

[5] St. Teresa of Avila. *The Life of Teresa of Jesus*, Chapter XXIX. 1565. Translated by E. Allison Peers, 1943.

[6] Pope Benedict XVI. "Deus Caritas Est." 25 December 2005. w2.vatican.va/content/benedict-xvi/en/encyclicals/documents/hf_ben-xvi_enc_20051225_deus-caritas-est.html. Accessed 27 February 2019.

[7] Goodstein, Laurie. Obituary of Billy Graham. *NY Times*, 21 February 2018.

[8] St. John Chrysostom. www.goodreads.com/quotes/167424-helping-a-person-in-need-is-good-in-itself-but. Accessed 27 February 2019.

[9] St. Teresa of Calcutta. www.goodreads.com/quotes/9401-do-not-think-that-love-in-order-to-be-genuine. Accessed 27 February 2019.

[10] St. Teresa of Calcutta. *The Simple Path.* Penguin Random House, 1995.

[11] St. Teresa of Calcutta (quoted by Pope Francis). "Why the Only Future Worth Building Includes Everyone." *Ted,* April 2017. www.ted.com/talks/pope_francis_why_the_only_future_worth_building_includes_everyone. Accessed 27 February 2019.

Chapter 10

[1] St. Augustine. *Confessions*, Book 1, Chapter 1. 401.

[2] "Cheryl Steed: Can Altruism Be Learned?" *Ted Radio Hour*, 26 May 2017. www.npr.org/templates/transcript/transcript.php?storyId=529957902. Accessed 27 February 2019.

[3] Turley, K.V. "The Final Hours of Jacques Fesch." *Crisis Magazine*, 5 December 2014.

[4] Merton, T. *The Seven Story Mountain*. Harcourt Brace, 1948.

[5] St. Thomas Aquinas. *On Kingship: To the King of Cypress.* 1267. Translated by G. Phelan, 1949.

[6] St. Teresa of Calcutta. www.goodreads.com/quotes/16809-god-doesn-t-require-us-to-succeed-he-only-requires-that. Accessed on 27 February 2019.

Made in the USA
Columbia, SC
03 June 2019